PAPAL POWER

ITS ORIGINS AND DEVELOPMENT

HENRY.T.HUDSON

D. C. Norrington.

11ᵗ·ˑ April, 2004.

 EVANGELICAL PRESS

EVANGELICAL PRESS
12 Wooler Street, Darlington, Co. Durham, DL1 1RQ.

© Evangelical Press 1981
First published 1981
Second impression 1983
Second edition 1989

ISBN 0 85234 269 1

Printed in Great Britain by The Bath Press, Avon.

DEDICATION

To all my beloved Italian friends who know
better than I could ever know what it is
like to live *sotto i Papi.*

Foreword

'The best pope is the worst pope,' thus affirmed Luther with regard to the papal institution, upon which rests the government of Roman Catholicism.

This affirmation of Luther is not an expression of the Reformer's personal opinion with regard to the person and the conduct of one of the Roman pontiffs, but the expression of a radical judgement of condemnation upon the papal institution itself, an institution which, in its form and in its character, is not based on any apparent instruction in the Scriptures, but rather is in open contrast with them.

For Luther, involved as he was in the recalling of Christendom to a rediscovery of the Word of God as being the one and only authority in matters of faith and conduct, this contrast was more than sufficient for him to express the aforementioned severe judgement of condemnation on the papacy.

Many evangelical believers of our time no longer seem to hold a similar consistent view of the relation between the Scriptures, faith and knowledge. For this reason, the evangelicals of our time can best be described as having but 'little power' (Revelation 3:8), barely sufficient to carry forward in some way the mandate of evangelization, but not sufficient to put to the test 'them who say they are apostles, and are not,' and to find them liars (Revelation 2:2).

In times like these, I am delighted with the decision of Dr Henry T. Hudson, to write and to publish a work on the origins and the development of papal power.

When the television charisma and the public relations of

the present Roman pontiff appear to exercise an influence over the convictions and the sentiments of so many evangelical believers, particularly in the United States (an influence seemingly more persuasive than that exercised by the Scriptures), it is providential that a book such as this should seek to make known the history and the nature of the papal institution in the light of the Scriptures.

Evangelicals cannot do less than lay hold of such knowledge, if they want to accept in earnest the responsibility to communicate the liberating power of the gospel 'first' to Roman Catholics, 'and also' to everyone else (Romans 1:16).

Moreover, this knowledge will have the beneficial effect of protecting the evangelical churches from the peril of producing, or of listening to leaders who are not completely submissive to the authority of the Word of God.

Indeed, even if the awakening of the Reformation has been, and is, a vaccine remarkably effective in the face of papal tendencies, the danger of the reappearance of this sickness in other more extenuating forms is ever present.

I believe that the labour of Dr Hudson has been determined not only by his love for the truth, but also by the love which he has for the believers and the people of Italy, whose lot it is to live under the nefarious influence of the Vatican City State and its king.

For this affection towards the people of my country, I want to thank Dr Hudson, and I want to assure him that in the hearts of the Italian evangelical believers there has always been a particular place for all those who, like him, have understood and sought to share the implications of the duty entrusted to us by God to proclaim and to live the gospel in this country.

Elio Milazzo
President, Italian Evangelical Alliance
Florence, Italy

Introduction

'JOHN PAUL, SUPERSTAR'. So read the front cover of *Time* magazine dated 15 October 1979. Journalistic exaggeration? Perhaps, but to judge from the TV coverage and the public printed news media, the impression was given that the greater part of the population of the United States had turned to Roman Catholicism during the first week of October 1979. By any earthly standards, the pope's visit was a smash hit! He spoke before the United Nations. He captured nationwide television. He was honoured with a White House reception and a private meeting with the presidential family. Senator Ted Kennedy did not hesitate to kiss his ring in public. Headlines such as 'JEWS AND PROTESTANTS LAUD VISIT' appeared in major newspapers. David Sanford, managing editor of *Harper's*, wrote that 'It was a collective act unrivalled in the annals of crowd psychology since the Beatles . . .'[1] In a footnote Sanford expanded this observation with the somewhat facetious comment: 'The pope is more popular than the Beatles, who, according to John Lennon, were more popular than Jesus; where this leaves Jesus is not clear.'[2] Moreover, before concluding, he exclaimed, 'I cannot remember a news event in which so much that was said and written by professional journalists contained so much puffery.'[3]

The phenomenon of the pope's visit will no doubt provide much fuel for psycho-sociological analysis for some time to come. How can anyone begin to explain his widespread

1

popular reception? Whatever happened to the traditional anti-papal sentiments common in American history? The early colonists and the Founding Fathers were predominantly progeny from Reformed Protestantism.[4] By and large they were outspokenly anti-papal. This propensity was evident throughout the nineteenth, and on into the twentieth century. What then brought about the change? Perhaps one reporter came closer to the answer than he realized when he wrote, 'Nobody is prejudiced any more because nobody takes [religion] that seriously: you have to believe in something first to be bigoted.'[5] Be all this as it may, I found it to be no small coincidence that the commotion connected with the pope's visit should take place at the same time that I began looking over my manuscript for this book. However, this was by no means the main reason for the interest in my subject, although I must admit it spurred my desire to see the result of my research published and presented to a wider audience.

My initial interest in studying the origins and the development of papal power reaches back at least two decades to the several years of my life which were spent in Italy. The experiences which derive from living there — that is, actually residing among the Italian people, going about the normal daily routines of life in much the way they would — produce an altogether different diary of observations and impressions from that which might be reported by any two-week-overnight-turned-expert tourist. In this regard, the words of Luigi Barzini are pungent. He wrote, 'The Italian way of life cannot be considered a success except by temporary visitors. It solves no problems. It makes them worse.'[6] In fact, not only do 'temporary visitors' tend to misread the complex cultural expressions of life in Italy, but I have noticed that they sometimes are among the first to object to any firsthand insights that might be shared. That in itself is somewhat of a key to the enigmatical nature of the Italian way of life. Superficiality and reality become easily confused. 'Unless you live there,' wrote Morris West, 'it is impossible to believe how crazy the country can be, how precarious are the foundations upon which it rests.'[7]

West, while writing on a different subject from the one which interests me, nevertheless includes among the foundations of modern Italy an inheritance of stupidity built into the system by — among other historical forces — 'absolutist popes'. Most assuredly, the Italy of yesterday and the Italy of today cannot be appreciated in any fair degree without some reference to the pervasive power of the papacy. The longer I lived there, and the more I came to understand the various facets of the overall culture, the more I began to realize just how extensive was this power. That such a condition does prevail is not difficult to comprehend. The papacy, as most people are well aware, is the governing body of the Roman Catholic Church, and according to a number of religious census statistics, more than ninety-four per cent of the Italian population belong to that church.

Some form of personal relationship with the Roman church is almost indispensable for survival and success in Italy. This might seem like a sweeping generalization, but Barzini, discussing the role of organizational structures which promote security and advancement in Italian society, began with the church, 'the oldest and largest of all . . . a State within a State . . .'. He described the 'holy Roman Catholic Church' as 'the greatest flowering of the Italian political genius'. So pervasive is the influence of this enormous religio-political organization in the life of an average Italian that, 'It can accompany him, step by step, from birth to death, assuring him a good job and a steady career, protecting him from the envy of rivals, procuring for him, at times, worldly success, fame, political power and wealth.'[8]

In all likelihood, some readers will do little more than blink over such observations. However, because I know by immediate involvement something of the frustrations of life in Italy, I cannot help but be troubled by them. For me, they bear disturbing implications. For example, how do I reconcile what is taught in the Bible about the social impact of the Christian faith upon any given society and the quality of life in Italy? Admittedly, a similar question might be raised with reference to any other land where the Christian church has a

solid foothold. But is there any other nation which can boast
a church membership of ninety-four per cent of the
population?

The Roman Catholic Church claims to be the true church
of Christ upon the earth, and the pope believes himself to be
the actual vicar of Jesus Christ. Imagine what a Muslim or a
Buddhist might think about Christianity, should they happen
to be direct observers of Italian life! Would they have any
way of knowing that visible ecclesiastical power and true
Christianity are not necessarily one and the same thing? Yet
who could really fault them, should they entertain the notion
that there is some cause-and-effect relationship between the
power and influence of the Roman church and the Italian
way of life? Certainly, such a judgement is frequently made
by Western minds with regard to Muslim countries where
similar percentages prevail. Why not here? At best, the
influence of the Roman church for the betterment of the
Italian people is negligible, and at worst, it may well be a
direct contributor to the debilitating impossibilities of their
daily frustrations. This latter alternative has been ably
argued by a number of qualified observers, beginning as
early as Machiavelli. What is more, there have been those
who, having at one time been fervent Roman Catholics, have
nevertheless been led to view the Roman church as 'the
antithesis of Christianity'.[9]

Of course, there is always the question as to the actual
extent of the influence of religion upon any given society.
And, admittedly, that is not easy to measure. However,
quite frankly, I believe only a prejudiced fool, or perhaps one
blinded by the reflex of modern secularism, would want to
argue that there is absolutely no correlation. One need only
think of events in Iran during 1979 to recognize that my
language is anything but exaggerated. The *de-facto* ruler,
and the power behind the Muslim forces which overthrew
the Shah, was the leading Shiite ayatollah, Ruholla
Khomeini. If anything, foreign policy failed to face up to
the effective force of religion in Iran.

Any number of reputable scholars could be cited who

accept the assumption that religion can, and does in effect produce a distinctive outlook on life. Two well-known examples in this regard, would be the sociological studies of Max Weber and R. H. Tawney.[10] Also, while not in the same category as these two studies, the observations of Alexis de Toqueville are worthy of consideration. De Toqueville wrote in the early half of the nineteenth century, and some of the things he observed with reference to the differences between religion in his native France and that of America serve well to illustrate what I am trying to say: for example, the distinction he made between a 'barren, traditionary faith which seems to vegetate' and that which lives in the soul.[11] He saw quite clearly, even as the Holy Scriptures so patently declare, that there is a world of difference between mere formalism in religion and the dynamic influence of sincere faith in God (Matthew 15:7—9; 23: 1—33).

Perhaps I ought to mention the fact that De Toqueville was a member of the Roman Catholic Church. His observations, therefore, can scarcely be discounted as those of a biased antagonist. If anything, they come across with greater significance. With this in mind, I would like to call attention to two other observations which bear upon the point that I am trying to make. First, after acknowledging that the greatest part of British America had been peopled by men who had shaken off the authority of the pope, De Toqueville told his readers that in America, in contrast to the way it was in France, the spirit of religion and the spirit of freedom marched together in close accord. By implication, his expression of astonishment at this phenomenon reveals more to a perceptive reader than does his proffered explanation. However, in his explanation — and this is the second observation— he traced the cause to the principle of separation of church and state. Obviously, from his remarks, he considered this 'new state of things' to be a great blessing.[12] In other words, De Toqueville was persuaded that nothing but detrimental consequences can follow in any society where religion is permitted to be prostituted to further political ends.

But I am drifting slightly off my subject. Let me return to what prompted this study in the first place. So far, in essence, what I have suggested is that during my residence in Italy I was disturbed by a disconcerting paradox. On the one hand, there was a powerful ecclesiastical system permeating most facets of Italian society and supposedly representing the church of Christ upon the earth, and on the other hand, a quality of life which appeared to contradict so much of that for which Christianity stands. Were my sentiments totally without reason? Had not the Lord Jesus Christ Himself said, 'A good tree cannot bring forth evil fruit . . . Wherefore by their fruits ye shall know them'? (Matthew 7:18, 20.) But beyond this disquieting inconsistency, there was one further matter which prodded me in the direction of a study dealing with the origins and growth of papal power. It was the greatness of papal power itself. And, in certain respects, this particular question bothered me more than the paradox I have already described.

In very obvious ways, the greatness and the power of the papacy are more apparent in the city of Rome than possibly in any other place in the world. This fact becomes particularly noticeable when one visits St Peter's Basilica and Vatican City. I would suppose that I have visited the so-called papal state (land area of just over 100 acres) at least a dozen times. Most of these visits were made at the request of friends who had enlisted my services as a kind of tour guide to help direct them through what are unquestionably some of the most beautiful artistic masterpieces in the world. Who, with any degree of aesthetic taste, could fail to appreciate the breath-taking marvels crowded within the five-mile labyrinth of buildings which houses no less than thirteen museums? Little wonder that the faces of the tourists reflect the agog state of their minds. They are walking through corridor after corridor of priceless art exhibits. In certain respects, I myself am no different. Every time I have viewed the Vatican art treasures, I have sensed inexpressible wonderment. This is especially true when my eyes try to take in what is probably the centre-piece of all, Michelangelo's work on the ceiling of the Sistine Chapel.

However, my own appreciation has always been tempered by mixed emotions. On almost every occasion, particularly as I walked around the inside of St Peter's Basilica, my soul has been troubled by a single question. In order to grasp the force of the question, it is perhaps necessary to try to imagine the scene. I am standing somewhere in the central nave near Bernini's massive canopy which covers the papal altar. From this vantage point, I can have a comprehensive view of much which makes up the grandeur of the largest church building in Christendom. Also from this same position, I can better observe the thousands of people who are milling around. For example, there is the seemingly endless line of people close by who are waiting to touch, or to kiss the extended toe of a black marble statue of Peter. Countless millions have performed this act of veneration, and the features of the toes have been virtually worn away. As my eyes take in all that is before me, my mind begins to ponder over the question: 'How can anyone relate all this to that which is set forth in the pages of the New Testament?' Were I to go through the crowds asking individuals this question, I would no doubt elicit a variety of responses, but on the whole, I would think that few would sympathize with my implied scepticism. As far as the majority appear to be concerned, I would venture to say that they harbour little, if any, doubt about there being a direct relationship between what they see and the basic teachings of Christianity. Of course, for most Italian Roman Catholics, it could hardly be otherwise. What they see has, in their minds, always been conterminous with Christianity. Furthermore, on the whole, they possess little, if any, firsthand knowledge of the content of Holy Scripture. This also could hardly be otherwise, since it has been, until only very recently, the consistent policy of the papal hierarchy to oppose the reading and study of the Bible, by both priests and laity.[13]

This then, the wide disparity between the straightforward teachings of the New Testament and the greatness and grandeur of the Roman papal church, became the cause of no small irritation to me. I felt sure that some kind of rational

explanation to the phenomenon could be found. My
academic background in both history and theology gave me
reason to believe that I could find it. My opinion that there
had to be some causative relationship between the centuries-
long dominating influence of the Roman church and the
'frustration and resigned discontent' of the Italian people
was another matter.[14] Limitations of time and ability pre-
cluded my becoming involved in such a comprehensive field
of study. So, leaving this latter problem, I took up the
former and, spurred primarily by the question of the
incredible gap between Holy Scripture and Roman papal
traditions, I began my research. Did I bridge the gap? The
following pages, for what they might be worth, contain the
answer.

NOTES

[1] David Sanford, 'The Pope's Groupies,' *Harper's*, Dec. 1979, vol. 259, no. 1555,
p. 86.
[2] *Ibid.*
[3] *Ibid.*, p. 89.
[4] Loraine Boettner estimated that approximately two-thirds of the entire population prior to 1776 were Reformed Protestants. Loraine Boettner, *The Reformed
Doctrine of Predestination* (Philadelphia: Presbyterian and Reformed Publishing
Co., 1974), pp. 382, 383.
[5] Sanford, *op. cit.*, p. 88.
[6] Luigi Barzini, *The Italians* (London: Hamish Hamilton, 1965), p. 339. The
quotation from Barzini comes in his concluding paragraph. In line with what
I tried to make plain to the reader, Barzini has another observation three pages
earlier which relates directly to this point: 'Foreign visitors are fascinated. They
are won over, as they have always been, by the "charm of Italy". Italian life is
gay, effervescent, intoxicating. The *dolce vita* looks now more *dolce* than it ever
was. Very few travellers see the ugliness underneath, the humiliation, the suffer-
ing. Not one in a hundred perceives the fundamental dreariness of everything
under the glittering ormolu, the bitter fate of men who are condemned peren-
nially to amuse themselves and the world, to hide their innermost feelings, to be
simpatici at all costs in order to make a living. What do they know of the peculiar
feeling of frustration and resigned discontent which paralyses the best Italians?'
(p. 336.)
[7] Morris West, 'Terror as an Historical Inheritance,' *Esquire*, 25 April 1978,
p.77.
[8] Barzini, *op. cit.*, pp. 220, 304.
[9] Alexander Robertson, *The Roman Catholic Church in Italy* (London: Morgan
and Scott, 1904), p. 88. Most theological libraries possess a wide assortment of
authors, beginning particularly from Luther's time, who have experienced such
a change of mind.

[10]Max Weber, *The Protestant Ethic and the Spirit of Capitalism* (New York, 1930), and R. H. Tawney, *Religion and the Rise of Capitalism* (New York, 1963).

[11]Alexis de Toqueville, *Democracy in America* (2 vols, New York, 1945), vol. I, p. 317.

[12]*Ibid.*, I, 311, 319, 322, *et passim*.

[13]One need only call to mind the words of Signor Guiseppe Zanardelli, Premier of Italy at the beginning of the twentieth century, in order to appreciate the profound significance of this point: 'Woe to the Roman Catholic Church when my countrymen get hold of the Old and New Testaments; then they will know the difference between Jesus Christ and His so-called vicar.' Robertson, *op. cit.*, p. 225.

[14]Barzini, *op. cit.*, p. 336.

1
The origins of papal power

The question of origins can be a very complicated matter. However, according to the traditions of Roman Catholic dogma, the source of papal power is traceable directly to Holy Scripture. An almost endless array of literary sources, particularly during the Middle Ages, could be cited in support of this claim. In effect, what this means is that the papal institution has been able to associate itself in an inextricable way with divine authority. In such a context, papal power becomes nothing short of the practical outworking of doctrinal concepts based upon sacred Scripture. If one should ask for a specific scriptural example to illustrate the association, in all likelihood Matthew 16:18, 19 would be given. Without any doubt, in this regard, this is the most quoted biblical passage of all. Proof of its importance becomes very evident to tourists visiting St Peter's Basilica in Rome. As they stand by the papal altar in the central nave and look up to admire Michelangelo's magnificent dome, they cannot fail to note the bold inscription around the base: *'Tu es Petrus, et super hanc petram aedificabo ecclesiam meam, et tibi dabo claves regni coelorum.'* ('Thou art Peter, and upon this rock I will build my church, and I will give unto thee the keys of the kingdom of heaven.')

'From these words,' according to Wladimir D'Ormesson, 'the papacy was born. They were to remain its basic charter through the centuries.'[1] By inference, the words were repeatedly proffered in support of two fundamental propositions: (1) Peter, as the rock upon whom the church would be built, was granted authoritative jurisdiction over all the followers of Jesus Christ, and (2) by what is known as 'apostolic succession', those who succeed Peter become the inheritors of this universal authority. Where is Rome mentioned in this text? Of course, it is not; but then it need not be, for the primacy of the Roman bishopric is derived from the claim that Peter was Bishop of Rome, and remained such till his death.[2] Granted the premises, the arguments for what has become known as 'the Petrine theory' are easy to follow. Those who succeed in the bishopric of Rome are the rightful heirs of Peter and therefore inherit the universal jurisdiction over the whole Christian church. There is, however, as any thoughtful person will quickly recognize, a wide gap between the words of Matthew 16:18 and the premises and deductions of Roman Catholic doctrine.

The mountain of literature produced by various exegetical studies of Matthew 16:18 is enormous.[3] That such should be the case is not hard to understand, since so much is at stake as far as papal claims to universal power are concerned. Among the early commentaries of the church fathers there was great diversity of opinion over the precise identity of the rock upon which the church would be built. One study made by a French Roman Catholic revealed the following facts: seventeen of the patristic writers said that Peter was the rock, forty-four were of the opinion that it was Peter's faith, sixteen favoured the view that the rock was Christ and eight said that it referred to all the apostles.[4] From those early writers, up till today, the interpretation of Matthew 16:18 has remained a major bone of contention.

During the Middle Ages, particularly the twelfth and thirteenth centuries, canon lawyers followed the 'well-worn grooves of patristic controversy in discussing the precise connotation of *super hanc petram'*.[5] If there was any shift in emphasis it was in the fact that the church was built principally upon Christ, and secondarily upon Peter. Differences of opinion were of no great consequence, since it was sufficient that the words of Matthew 16:18 at least permitted Peter some position of special importance. By this time in history, the whole Petrine theory was so well established that the mere fact of Peter's prominence constituted adequate evidence to support the theory. In later centuries, scholars might highlight the apparent logical fallacy which unwittingly reads the conclusion into the premise, but in the historical circumstances of the Middle Ages this was hardly possible. Papal power was *de facto* a reality. Matthew 16:18 provided a kind of divine corner-stone to the reality.

Thus, while the Petrine theory was inseparably associated with Matthew 16:18, it was not necessarily dependent upon the identification of Peter with the rock. For example, there were theologians such as Gabriel Biel who, as late as the fifteenth century, while yielding obedience to papal authority, nevertheless interpreted the rock to be Christ.[6] Incidentally, we might mention in passing that there have been Protestant expositors also who have opted for Peter's being the rock.[7] Obviously, then, the equation of Peter with the rock was not the equivalent of accepting papal views of power. However, as far as papal supporters were concerned, they were content merely to derive from Christ's words special eminence for Peter, which in itself tended to undergird the whole papal structure with great dignity and divine authority.

The controversy concerning the true identification of the rock, as important as it might be, should not be allowed to eclipse inquiry concerning the second proposition upon which the papacy stands, namely, the theory of apostolic succession. Does Matthew 16:18 support the claim that there was to be a perpetuation of authority and jurisdiction over the universal church through the line of bishops whose bishopric was located at Rome?[8] At the risk of sounding facetious, we would say that any affirmative answer to this question would indicate an extraordinary mode of exegesis. Obviously, no objective examination of the words could ever support the notion. Besides, the whole idea of universal authority, let alone apostolic succession, was far from accepted even some 600 years after the Lord spoke the words to Peter. Gregory the Great, 'servant of the servants of God', Bishop at Rome (590–604), had some pertinent

words on this matter. The Patriarch John IV of Constantinople had claimed the title of Universal Bishop, and
Gregory was prompted to declare that such a title was
'blasphemous, antichristian and diabolical, by whomsoever
assumed'.[9] Cyriacus, the successor of John IV, refused to
relinquish the title. However, Pope Boniface III (607) did
prevail upon the Emperor Phocas to take the title of
Ecumenical Bishop away from the Bishop of Constantinople,
and confer it upon the Roman bishop. Phocas' decision on
this matter was probably for no greater reason than that his
predecessor had taken a different position.

Edward Gibbon, in his illustrious history *The Decline
and Fall of the Roman Empire,* painted a villainous portrait
of Phocas. His succession to the throne took place in the
midst of great civil and military unrest. He was an obscure
centurion but, once holding the reins of power, he soon
manifested tyrannical cruelty. The five sons of the Emperor
Maurice were murdered before their parents' eyes. Then the
emperor himself was put to death. The bodies were cast
into the sea and their heads were displayed at Constantinople
till signs of putrefaction made disposal necessary. Shortly
afterwards, Phocas completed the 'massacre' of the imperial
family. The oldest son, Theodosius, who had been sent to
solicit help of the Persian monarch, was apprehended and was
beheaded at Nice. The mother and the three daughters were
executed at Chalcedon. Notwithstanding the monstrous
depravity of Phocas, Pope Gregory not only acquiesced to
the government of the usurper, but also applauded his
accession with base adulation, going so far as to call it 'a
glorious work of God'.[10]

Even with the aid of the notorious Phocas, the question of
a single bishop possessing authority and jurisdiction over the
whole church was by no means settled. The controversy eventually led to the rupture of Christendom in the ninth century. Papal supremacy came to be recognized only in the
Western half of the empire. There had been ecumenical
councils during the first five centuries; there were the many
ponderous volumes of the church fathers, but there is no

mention made of the doctrine of a Roman bishop reigning
as sovereign monarch over all the people of God. Such a
doctrine was apparently unknown during these early centuries. When compared with the papal claims of the
eleventh, twelfth and thirteenth centuries, this fact is somewhat difficult to explain. Is it possible that so momentous
a doctrine could have been taken for granted? The answer
could hardly be yes in the light of the controversy between
East and West, and in view of the nature of later extravagant
papal claims. How then did this doctrine gain such a solid
footing in the Western half of Christendom?

Surely, no one would want to argue that the great historical differences in the extent and power of the Roman see
between the sixth and twelfth centuries can be explained
solely by reference to the words of Matthew 16:18. Popes
such as Gregory VII (1073—1086), Innocent III (1198—
1216) and Boniface VIII (1294—1303) did, of course, appeal
to biblical passages, but the actual exercise of their power
can scarcely find valid explanation by reference to such
passages. Of necessity, a more acceptable explanation must
be sought somewhere in the milieu of historical forces and
events which bridge the period. Such recourse can hardly be
judged unreasonable. Little can be done for those who
ascribe everything to the direct intervention of God, and
who dismiss all discussion of intermediate causes. Such a
mentality would make the study of history a complete
waste of time. Yet, in certain ways, the Roman church is
almost forced into a conclusion of this sort with regard to
history, because from the perspective of later doctrinal
developments historical judgements could summarily be
invalidated solely on the basis of ecclesiastical authority.[11]

The relationship between the Roman church and history
poses some interesting problems. As has just been suggested,
such doctrines as the primacy and universal jurisdiction of
the Roman popes are not derived from explicit statements
of Holy Scripture. The same might be said for the dogma
of papal infallibility which was promulgated in 1870. Most
modern Roman Catholic scholars will frankly admit this

fact. If, then, there is no single text or series of texts anywhere in the Bible to prove these doctrines, from whence
did they come? Self-evidently they reflect a post-biblical
development which, of course, means that they were introduced at a particular point in history to meet the needs of
certain groups within the church. This does not imply that
they have absolutely no connection with Scripture. In the
words of one Roman Catholic scholar they resulted from
a discernible 'trajectory' of biblical images. With reference
to the doctrine of infallibility, the trajectory was truly
amazing, reaching all the way from the first to the nineteenth century. When it was promulgated, it was declared
to be a doctrine which belonged to 'the ancient and constant faith of the church'.[13] Here, then, is a problem of
first magnitude, for as far as Scripture is concerned the
doctrine was totally alien to the early church.

In the nineteenth century controversy concerning papal
infallibility, there seemed to be no doubt that the dogma,
once proclaimed, would greatly enhance the position and
power of the pope. How anyone could possibly imagine
the papacy being more exalted, or more powerful than it
was in the Middle Ages is difficult to conceive. Yet, nevertheless, there was a widespread opinion that it would
constitute a sort of Magna Carta of ecclesiastical absolutism.
In some way or other it was viewed as being the other side
of the coin of supreme jurisdiction. However, the juxta-
position of the two concepts cannot signify anything less
than the conquering of history by theology, for as far as
historical judgements are concerned, infallibility and
sovereignty are intrinsically incongruous. By definition,
according to the Vatican Council itself, infallible decrees
are irreformable. The binding of a 'sovereign' ruler by the
irreformable acts of his predecessors is historically un-
thinkable. Furthermore, the same paragraph which defines
the infallibility of the Roman pontiff states that in promul-
gating the dogma, the council was 'adhering to the tradition
received from the beginning of the Christian faith . . .'.[14]
One might wonder how this can be, since the concept of

the infallibility of the pope does not appear in the New
Testament. It must lie somewhere along the 'trajectory' of
history, which means that historians must research a complex concatenation of historical circumstances in order to
discover how the tradition was started in the first place.
According to the work of Brian Tierney (*Origins of Papal
Infallibility, 1150—1350*, Leiden: Brill, 1972), the doctrine
emerged in the years around 1300. Of course, it did not
appear out of thin air. Papal power must have achieved
such heights that a doctrinal claim of so great a consequence
could be argued seriously. How then did such power come
into existence? Obviously, the historical dimensions to the
question cannot be avoided.

As has been noted, the first five centuries of Christianity
knew little or nothing about an actual supreme rulership
of the Roman pope over all churches. What then, from a
historical point of view, could make such an unprecedented
claim possible? One plausible answer has been suggested by a
number of historians. It is that there seems to be a definite
correlation between the power vacuum created by the demise
of the ancient Roman civilization and the growth and
development of papal power at Rome.   Francesco
Guicciardini (1482—1540), in his classic history of the
Italian Renaissance, was clearly of this opinion. He claimed
that nobody denied 'that the transfer of the imperial seat
to Constantinople was the first origin of papal power'. As
a result of the transfer, the Roman pontiffs were left free of
imperial control and they themselves began to assume temporal power. Thomas Hobbes (1588—1679), in his *Leviathan,*
described the papacy as 'no other than the ghost of the
deceased *Roman Empire,* sitting crowned upon the grave
thereof. For so did the papacy start up on a sudden out of
the ruins of that heathen power.'[15] Call it a historical acci-
dent, if there be such a thing, but clearly, in the time-space
continuum of historical happenings, responsibilities of a
more secular nature were thrust upon the church. These
may not have been desired by any of the Bishops of Rome,
but the historical turn of events could hardly have been

avoided. 'In the West' there was 'the gradual disintegration of all effective imperial authority' which 'made possible the growth of a quite different tradition'.[16] In the words of another writer, 'The popes reluctantly took over the role of the Caesars.'[17] In effect, 'the church came to be the new incarnation of Roman unity'.[18] The transition is not that difficult to understand, for the church was the only institution strong enough to provide necessary leadership.[19]

A further contributing factor, which eventually led to the growth and extension of papal power, was the Emperor Constantine's acceptance of Christianity, and the problems that this entailed. Christianity became the religion of the empire. The Bishop of Rome had the prestige of association with the imperial metropolis of the world. Before long, questions concerning the relationship between church and state elicited no small controversy. Both were looked upon as being ordained of God and each was granted certain powers within its own respective jurisdiction. For example, Constantine assumed responsibility for the external administration of the church and left the internal supervision to the bishops. The division seemed reasonable, but with the passing of time theoretical boundaries became blurred and the bishops began to pre-empt the advantage of the spiritual estate over the consciences of men. An illustration of how this was argued by the bishops can be seen in the letter of Pope Gelasius (492–496) to the Emperor Anastasius.

'There are indeed, most august Emperor, two powers by which this world is chiefly ruled: the sacred authority of the popes and the royal power. Of these the priestly power is much more important, because it has to render account for the kings of men themselves at the divine tribunal. For you know, our very clement son, that although you have the chief place in dignity over the human race, yet you must submit yourself faithfully to those who have charge of divine things and look to them for the means of your salvation.'[20]

In theory, the basis for the later more exorbitant papal claims of authority over the temporal power was therefore

present as early as the fifth century. The subsequent centuries tell a tale of the see-sawing action of the struggle for
prominence between the two. What may have sounded
acceptable in theory did not necessarily prove so in practice.
In one voluminous work which deals with this problem in
great detail, attention is directed to what in effect did
actually happen.

'The powers were co-ordinate, and, in their own spheres,
independent of each other. But, as a matter of fact, circumstances were too strong for theory, and not only did the
definition and delimitation of the boundaries of the province
of each power prove a task of insuperable difficulty, but
each power in turn found itself compelled to trench in
some measure upon the province of the other.'[21]

By the time of the later Middle Ages there could be little
doubt which power was trenching the most. When compared with the earlier centuries, the extent of the later papal
claims appear incredible. It was not simply a matter of the
pope's jurisdiction being limited to the clergy and to spiritual
matters, for that was generally conceded, but it was that
'omnes subsunt ei jure divine' (everybody is subject to his
jurisdiction), *'parem non habet super terram'* (nor has he
any equal on earth).[22] Such claims recur repeatedly in
canonistic writings, and as Walter Ullman wrote, they 'have
to be taken literally: the idea of hyperbole was foreign to
the canonists'.[23]

According to Ullman, the controversy 'papacy versus
empire' was analogically related to the ancient antagonism
between mind and matter: 'Just as the soul is superior to
the body, in the same way the pope is superior to the
emperor.'[24] It was Aristotle who had taught that the spiritual
was something divine and, therefore, the most valuable and
the most distinctive of man's attributes. Relating this to the
spiritual and temporal powers, the conclusion falls logically
in favour of the spiritual being the more important. There
were, then, philosophical, biblical and historical reasons for
exalting the pope above the emperor.[25] These reasons were
carefully mustered and masterfully applied in the papal

claims which emanated from the Roman see during the Middle Ages.

Also, in order to bolster these claims. a number of remarkable forgeries came into existence. One of them, the *Donation of Constantine*, laid the foundation for the territorial claims of the papacy. In the *Donation*, the pope and the clergy were bequeathed the privileges which had belonged to the emperor. The significance of the transaction is important, for it highlighted the claim that the temporal was inferior to the spiritual. It also provided a theoretical base to rest papal power upon human as well as divine law.[26] More will be said about such forgeries in dealing with the development of papal power. For the moment, let it be noted that such documents were apparently accepted quite readily by Gratian (*circa* 1140), the founder of the science of canon law. In citing from the popes of the first four centuries, he is reported to have taken 313 out of 324 quotations directly from these forgeries.[27] In all probability, however, these forgeries were less vital than one might be led to think. Certainly they were useful in propping up papal claims, but they were merely addenda to a tradition that was already entrenched in the minds of papal supporters.

Further discussion of the question of the origins of papal power hardly seems necessary. What has been said is sufficient to form an intelligent appreciation of its theoretical and historical foundations. When it comes to the consideration of the development of papal power, there will, of course, be some overlapping, which will shed additional light on this first chapter. Also, in the following chapters, the discussion will reach to the Vatican Councils of 1870 and 1963–65. From all this, the reader will be able to apprehend whether or not there have been any significant changes in the Roman Catholic hierarchy as to the nature and the extent of papal power. At this point, what might be helpful is a brief summarization of what has been stated with regard to origins. As mentioned at the beginning, the question of origins is not an easy matter in historical study. However, when we look at papal power from the perspective of the

Middle Ages, there does seem to be a detectable combination of interdependent factors which account for its historical manifestation.

First of all, out of the circumstances surrounding the disintegration of the Western half of the empire, the Roman church emerged as the only structure strong enough to provide some degree of unity. It was not, therefore, unusual that the bishop of the largest city of the empire should be thrust into a position of prominence. He had no rival to speak of in the West. His see was comparatively free of strife and heresy. He was also at various times called upon to mediate in theological disputes which were even outside his own jurisdictional limits. Added to these considerations, his see had the traditional distinction of being associated with the illustrious name of the apostle Peter, and this association, more than anything, tied to the doctrine of apostolic succession, became the theoretical corner-stone in the development of papal power throughout the Middle Ages. So then, the historical circumstances of the first five centuries provided the soil in which a complex mixture of biblical, philosophical, theological and legal seeds took root. From these grew a nondescript plant which claimed to be quasi-divine in nature. In essence, in the words of J. B. Lightfoot, 'the power of the Bishop of Rome was built upon the power of the church of Rome. It was originally a primacy, not of the episcopate, but of the church.'[28] The same thesis, slightly more elaborate, is repeated by Walter Ullman: 'Because it was situated in the capital of the Roman Empire, the local *Roman* church had a special pre-eminence and superior authority, and its agreement to any ecclesiastical or religious measure proposed was for this very reason held to be essential in the interests of the *Roman* Empire. This position accorded to the Roman church by the imperial government to no small extent fertilized the ground for the later juristic pre-eminence and primacy of the Roman church.'[29]

NOTES

[1] Wladimir D'Ormesson, *The Papacy*, trans. Michael Derrick, vol. 81 of the *Twentieth Century Encyclopedia of Catholicism*, ed. Henri Daniel Rops (New York: Hawthorne Books, 1959), p. 10.

[2] Wladimir D'Ormesson considers Peter's presence at Rome to be crucial with respect to the founding of the papacy. (*Ibid.,* p. 27.) Protestant champions have attempted to prove that Peter never was at Rome. If it is possible to prove a negative at all, then it may be concluded, at least with a high degree of probability, that he was not at Rome during any of the time covered by the history of the canonical Scriptures. He may have suffered martyrdom at Rome, but the tradition of a twenty-five year episcopate can hardly be maintained unless, of course, he was an absentee bishop. The traditional dates for his episcopate are from A.D. 41 to 66. Consider the following facts.

In 44 he was imprisoned in Jerusalem (Acts 12).

In 52 he was at the Council of Jerusalem (Acts 15).

In 53 Paul joined him at Antioch (Galatians 2).

In 58 Paul wrote to the Romans, but does not mention him. In Romans 1.11, he wants to impart special gifts, and in Romans 1.15 he is ready to preach there. He sends greetings to twenty-seven persons, but none to Peter.

In 61 Paul is conveyed a prisoner to Rome, and certain brethren go to meet him, but not Peter.

At Rome Paul writes to the Galatians, and mentions Peter, but not as being there or as having been pontiff there for twenty years.

The Epistles to the Ephesians, Philippians, Colossians and Philemon were all written from Rome; but while others are mentioned as sending messages, or as being associated with Paul, Peter is never once mentioned.

From Rome also Paul's last letter is written (the Second Epistle to Timothy). He says, 'At my first answer no man stood with me, but all men forsook me' (2 Timothy 4:16). So that if Peter were Bishop of Rome he enjoyed an immunity which was not accorded to Paul, and is guilty of having forsaken the great apostle.

And, finally, in this very Epistle, written from Rome immediately before his martyrdom, Paul says, 'Only Luke is with me' (2 Timothy 4:11). This is conclusive.

So Paul had written to Rome, he had been in Rome, and at the end he writes from Rome, and not only never once mentions Peter, but declares, 'Only Luke is with me.'

[3] The text of Matthew 16:18 is controverted over the interpretation of the Greek words *petros* and *petra*. An interlinear transliteration might be given as follows:

su ei Petros, kai epi taute te petra

Thou art Peter, and upon this the rock

oikodomeso mou ten ekklesian . . .

I will build of me the church . . .

A simple straightforward consideration of the grammatical construction seems to rule out Peter as the *petra*. We might paraphrase the text: 'Thou art Peter, a movable stone, but upon this, the immovable rock, I will build my church . . .' The theological implications of making Peter 'the immovable rock' would seem to be of serious consequences in the light of the context and Peter's later life. See Matthew 16:23; 26:69–75.

[4] George Salmon, *The Infallibility of the Church* (London: John Murray, 1914), p. 335.

[5] Brian Tierney, *Foundations of the Conciliar Theory* (Cambridge: University Press, 1955), p. 25.

[6] Heiko A. Oberman, *The Harvest of Medieval Theology* (Cambridge, Mass.: Harvard University Press, 1963), p. 413.

[7] William Smith, *Dictionary of the Bible* (4 vols., Boston: Houghton, Mifflin and Company, 1870), vol. III, p. 2448. See also Alfred Plummer, *An Exegetical Commentary of the Gospel of Matthew,* pp. 228—229. William L. Pettingil, *The Gospel of the Kingdom,* p. 203. Alfred Barnes, *An Explanatory and Practical Commentary on Matthew,* p. 170. John D. Davis, *The Westminster Dictionary of the Bible,* p. 473. James Hastings, *Dictionary of the Bible,* article on 'Peter'. Oscar Cullman, *Peter,* pp. 206—207. Marvin R. Vincent, *Word Studies in the New Testament,* vol. I, pp. 91—92.

[8] Even if one would accept the view that Peter is the rock, the 'Petrine theory' is surely still open to serious doubt. To what extent was Peter the leader of the apostles? (See Acts 15; Galatians 2.) Does the text really say that Peter was to have supreme authority, both legislative and judicial, over the whole church? Does it declare that this supposed authority is transmissible?

[9] Samuel G. Green, *A Handbook of Church History* (London: The Religious Tract Society, 1904), p. 344.

[10] Augustus Neander, *General History of the Christian Religion and Church,* trans. Joseph Torrey (10 vols, London: Henry G. Bohn, 1851), V, 156.

[11] John Emerich Edward Dalberg-Acton, *The History of Freedom and Other Essays* (New York: Books for Libraries Press, Inc., 1967), p. 515.

[12] Richard P. McBrien, *Catholicism* (2 vols; Minneapolis: Winston Press, Inc., 1980) II, 831, 832, 837.

[13] Geddes MacGregor, *The Vatican Revolution* (London: MacMillan & Co. Ltd., 1958), p. 169.

[14] *Ibid.,* p. 179.

[15] Francesco Guicciardini, *The History of Italy,* trans. Sidney Alexander (New York: The MacMillan Company, 1964), p. 143.

[16] Thomas Hobbes, *Leviathan* (New York: E. P. Dutton and Company, Inc., 1950), p. 614.

[17] Brian Tierney, *The Crisis of Church and State* (Englewood Cliffs, N. J., Prentice-Hall, Inc., 1964), p. 9.

[18] Norman F. Cantor, *Medieval History, the Life and Death of a Civilization* (New York: The MacMillan Company, 1964), p. 18.

[19] Roland H. Bainton, *Early and Medieval Christianity* (Boston: Beacon Press, 1962), p. 52.

[20] *Readings in Church History,* ed. Colman J. Barry (2 vols; Westminster, Maryland: The Newman Press, 1960), vol. I, 147.

[21] R. W. and A. J. Carlyle, *A History of Medieval Political Theory in the West* (6 vols; New York: Barnes and Noble, Inc., n.d.), vol. I, 284.

[22] Walter Ullmann, *Medieval Papalism, the Political Theories of the Medieval Canonists* (London: Methuen and Company, Ltd., 1949), p. 77.

[23] *Ibid.,* p. 77.

[24] *Ibid.,* p. 81.

[25] *Ibid.,* p. 176.

[26] *Ibid.,* pp. 108, 109.

[27] Hans Kung, *Infallible? An Enquiry,* trans. Erich Mosbacher (London: William Collins Sons & Co., Ltd., 1972), p. 95.
[28] J. B. Lightfoot, *The Apostolic Fathers* (London: 1890) part I, 70.
[29] Walter Ullman, *A Short History of the Papacy in the Middle Ages* (London: Methuen and Company, Ltd., 1972), p. 9.

2
The development before the Reformation

At the outset, there is once again the problem of origins. Where does one turn to find what might indisputably be considered the first historical manifestation of the exercise of papal power? Even the use of the title 'Pope' did not belong exclusively to the Roman bishop. E. Giles in his *Documents Illustrating Papal Authority A.D. 96–454,* cited archaeological evidence for the earliest use of *Papa* for the Bishop of Rome as belonging to the beginning of the fourth century. He pointed out also that the Bishop of Carthage and the Bishop of Alexandria were both called 'Pope' at least fifty years earlier.[1] Perhaps, as some church historians have suggested, the first glimmer of 'papal' power is to be found in the letter of Clement, the third Bishop of Rome, to the church at Corinth (95 A.D.?).[2] However, such a conclusion can only be deduced by inference and is somewhat doubtful. Clement did not really assert jurisdictional authority, rather, the tenor of his letter was clearly that of spiritual concern for the feuding Christians at Corinth, and he rebuked them for their unruly behaviour.[3] By analogy this would be little different from any pastor writing to admonish Christian brethren in a church other than his own. Certainly it would not mean lordship over them.[4]

In point of time, the next reference that is generally cited to prop up papal claims comes from Ignatius the Bishop of Antioch (III). In writing to the church of Rome, he wrote of 'her that hath the presidency in the country of the region of the Romans . . .'[5] If anything, Ignatius' words, rather than proclaim the universal authority of the Bishop of Rome, do

24

little more than circumscribe the limits of jurisdiction exercised by the church at Rome. A better case for papal supremacy can be made from the writings of Irenaeus (130–200?). He wrote five books against the heresies of his day, and in his writings only one passage can be found which relates to the question of the primacy of the Roman see. Speaking of the Roman church, he exclaimed, 'For unto this church which holds a leading position among the churches must needs resort every church – that is the faithful who are everywhere – inasmuch as the apostolic tradition is always preserved by the faithful who are everywhere.'[6]

Here again, the subject matter and the context of the passage scarcely present the idea of a supreme *Cathedra Petri*. On the contrary, Irenaeus associated the Roman church with both Peter and Paul, and said nothing to give Peter the pre-eminence. Clearly his main concern was to lay stress upon apostolic tradition. Admittedly this would have been an ideal opportunity to spell out the case for the Petrine theory, but he did not do so. The context makes plain that he was arguing that the Roman church was founded by Peter and Paul, therefore the faithful resort to her. The fact that the Roman church held 'a leading position among the churches' in no way meant that the Roman bishop was head over all the churches. Later popes, conveniently dropping out Paul, nevertheless used the apostolic association to further their claims to absolute supremacy.

A further case, somewhat doubtful in point of authenticity, yet one which became a substantial foundation-stone in the building of papal pretensions, is made from the canons of the Council of Sardica (346). They were only applicable in the West and, even if genuine, they by no means recognized papal supremacy. What they granted was an appellate jurisdiction to the see of Rome. Before this time no provision had been made for an appeal from a provincial synod for a bishop who felt himself wronged. In similar vein, the Emperor Valentinian enacted a law in 372, 'empowering the Bishop of Rome to examine and judge other bishops, that religious disputes might not be decided by profane or secular judges'.[7] It is not surprising, therefore, that the Bishops of Rome, armed with the prestige of 'double apostolicity' and with the position of appellate authority, should become imbued with the belief that their authority was supreme over the whole church.

The expression 'the apostolic see' was applied to the bishopric of Rome by Pope Damasus in 378. It is a totally unbiblical conception. The powers of the apostles were extraordinary and incompatible with the limitations of a local see. How could any apostle, let alone Peter, be viewed within the confines of a local pastorate without neglecting his apostolic duties? Notwithstanding this question, the term was adopted without any apparent opposition. It was used by Augustine around 416. However, he did not use it to support the doctrine of papal supremacy. To quote him as having said, '*Roma locuta est, causa finita est*' (Rome has spoken, the case is ended) distorts the truth. Clearly, he viewed the pope's decision as being only one element in the combined witness of the Western church.[8] But he did allow the equation of expressions between 'Roman see' and 'apostolic see'. All that was now needed was for someone to join together 'primacy' and 'apostolic see'. This was done by Boniface I in 422, and was given permanent fixation by Leo I (440–461). Leo reasoned that since Christ commissioned Peter, and since he alone was vicar of St Peter, that same jurisdictional power which was given to Peter must be his also.

The extent to which Leo's claims were acknowledged remains a debatable point. By the fifth century, the Roman see held a high position of respect. As was pointed out, it had been granted an appellate status over other bishops by imperial law. Yet, the details concerning the exercise of this authority reveal some interesting facts. Take the case of Apriarius, for example. He was an African priest who had been deposed by his bishop. He appealed to Pope Zosimus (417–418) and again to Pope Celestine (422–432). The appeals sparked controversy. This fact clearly implies that there was no general recognition of papal supremacy. But more than this, during the controversy something happened which singularly underscores the absence of total submission to the Roman bishop. Citations from the canons of the Council of Nicaea (325) made it apparent that jurisdictional authority was understood to be limited, and not universal. Incidentally, as Ullman pointed out, the church of Rome did not even play a minor part in this great Council of Nicaea, even though in later years it was given credit for the leadership of this council.[9]

At the Council of Ephesus (431) a small papal legation of three representatives was present. There they expressed the opinion that St Peter was the chief of the apostles, the veritable foundation-stone of the universal church, and that his successor was the pope in Rome. This declaration re-appeared in countless papal documents from the fifth century to Vatican I in 1870. Yet despite these claims, the papal legation played a negligible role at the council. Even at the Council of Chalcedon (451), where Pope Leo's position was given exalted recognition, there was also undeniable limitation of his jurisdictional authority. For one thing, it passed canons which maintained the rights of synods to act independently of Rome. It also awarded equal rights and privileges to Constantinople such as the fathers had assigned to Rome. When the Roman legates heard of this decision they objected. They produced a version of the Canon of Nicaea which claimed, *'Ecclesia Roman semper habuit principatum'* (The Roman church has always had the headship). They were confronted with the Greek original, and the claim was repudiated. They were apparently unaware that the words had been added at Rome. With regard to the matter of papal legates from Rome, the twenty-ninth Council of Carthage (424) had objected, asking, 'Was it held that the illumination of the Holy Spirit had been reserved for a single person [the pope], and denied to great assemblies of bishops?'[10]

In spite of such conciliar objections, it seems apparent that the foundational groundwork for the edifice of papal power was laid during the fifth century. Also at this time, mixed into the conceptual concrete of these foundations were some literary productions which were nothing more than legends and forgeries. The first, which served to reinforce later papal claims to temporal power, was the *Legend of St Silvester,* which appeared between 480 and 490. The intent of its unknown author was to highlight the role of Pope Silvester (314—336) in influencing Constantine to create a new capital of the empire. The credit for raising Constantinople to its pre-eminent position therefore went to the papacy. In one scene, the writer depicted Constantine, without his imperial symbols of office, lying prostrate before Silvester. After this act of contrition, Constantine was reinvested with his emperor's emblems and soon thereafter moved his capital to Constantinople. There was, of course, not one scintilla of truth in the whole story yet, nevertheless, it held such sway that by the eighth century it was incorporated into the more influential forgery known as the *Donation of Constantine.* In this later document, Constantine, before departing to Constantinople, supposedly bestowed upon Silvester vast regions of land in the Western half of the empire.

Before the fifth century ended, further literary undergirdings of papal power saw the light of day. They were conceived in the midst of a papal schism between two candidates for the papal chair. Interestingly, the two factions, acting independently of each other, held their elections on the same day and almost at the same time. Symmachus won the day over Laurentius — not because of amicable concessions, but because of the intervention of the Gothic King Theodoric who sided with Symmachus. The factional fighting gave rise to a number of forgeries, which specialized in the invention of synods. One of the Symmachan forgeries contained speeches made at an imaginary synod during the reign of Diocletian (284—305). Another described a synod headed by Pope Silvester in which Constantine also took part. The whole point of the so-called *Symmachan Apocrypha* was to weave together historical and fictional details so that they would fit into the contemporary events lending support to the papal claims of Symmachus. One example of the nature of this support comes from the imaginary council that was chaired by Silvester. It comes in the form of a decree which stated that 'Nobody can sit in judgement on the first (apostolic) see which distributes rightful justice to all. Neither the emperor nor the whole clergy nor kings nor people can judge the supreme judge.'[11] The importance of these forgeries can be seen in that they were later incorporated into a number of collections of canon law, and thus became part of the official body of Roman Catholic tradition. They added to the mystique of prestige which made possible the more extravagant papal claims of the later Middle Ages.

It might be argued that, even without the legends and forgeries, the prestige of the Roman church would have continued to grow. Historical circumstances were all in its favour. It was only to be expected that the bishop of the first city be considered the first bishop in the church. To be expected? Yes, perhaps to the bishop of the first city, but as has been noted, not necessarily to all other bishops. At Chalcedon it had been decreed that Constantinople should be equal to Rome in status. From the Eastern half of the empire there was granted a kind of condescending see-sawing primacy of respect, but not of actual jurisdiction. The shift of political prominence from Rome to Constantinople had caused a commensurate shift in emphasis with regard to papal claims. No longer could there be any claim of primacy by way of association with the capital city. If political status determined ecclesiastical status, then Constantinople would gain the ascendancy. The Roman answer to this threat was to shift the emphasis to claims based upon the Petrine theory. However, even in the face of this new emphasis, the Eastern ecclesiastics failed to grant undisputed jurisdictional primacy.

From chapter 1, it will be remembered that the controversy over which bishop was the ecumenical bishop was still going strong at the end of the sixth century. Notwithstanding this fact, the fifth century seems to be the time when a distinct regal-sacerdotal concept of papal power began to be formed. For example, this seems to be nascent in the letter which Pope Gelasius wrote to the Emperor Anastasius, which was also mentioned in chapter 1. The Gelasian theses implied a subtle monarchical-type conception: 'The pope as successor of St Peter has sole [authority] over the corporate body of Christians, amongst whom the emperor takes indeed a vital place, but one of an assistant nature . . .'[12] Not all popes in the fifth century shared Gelasius' viewpoint. If anything, his importance in the development of papal power comes more into focus in the later Middle Ages when propagandists used his theses to support greater papal pretensions. In these early centuries there was some ambivalence with regard to the relationship between temporal and spiritual authority. Certain popes favoured a more conciliatory tone towards the East and others maintained the Gelasian hard line. Apparently, Pope Symmachus saw no inconsistency in writing intemperate letters to the emperor, while appealing for help to the Arian King Theodoric. Undoubtedly, geographical distance was a factor, for Italy was ruled by barbarian kings and the emperor was far away. But as the next two centuries reveal, the emperors did not allow distance or papal pretensions to offset their own claims to possessing the greater authority.

While the battle between the papacy and the empire was destined to sway back and forth during these early centuries, there was never any real doubt as to which held the field. In 482, the Emperor Zeno (474–491) drew up an imperial edict which became known by its formula of faith as the *Henotikon.* It was issued entirely on the emperor's own authority and it fixed the faith for the whole empire. The emperor viewed himself as the divinely appointed mouthpiece on the earth. There was a fusion of the sacred and the secular, which was in accordance with the tradition reaching back to Constantine (307–337), and even to the ancient Roman emperors. This combination of sacred and secular power gave rise to what came to be called 'Byzantine caesaropapism'. During the reign of Justinian I (527–565) the imperial theocracy reached a high peak. His granting of an exalted position to the papacy was really part of his plan to re-establish the Roman empire. It did not stop him from deposing Pope Silverius (536–537), who died in a penal colony, nor from imprisoning Pope Vigilius (537–555) and forcibly appointing Pope Pelagius I (556–561) as successor. By imperial decree Justinian fixed the legal procedure for papal elections.

Such matters did not, of course, halt the papal claims to be the successor of Peter, the foundation-stone of the universal church and the teacher and head of all orthodox Christians. But then neither did these claims prevent the continued harassment of the papacy by the empire. The Emperor Constans II (630–668) did not hesitate to bring Pope Martin I (649–655) to trial for charges of high treason. Martin I had been consecrated without imperial approval. He was tried and sentenced to death by quartering. The sentence was not carried out, but he was banished to the outmost limits of the empire there to die of privation. The stalwart faith of Martin I might be cause for admiration, but the episode nevertheless illustrates that it was the emperor who exercised supreme political and religious power over the Christian world of his day. However, this was by no means the last word in the struggle. In fact, as was already touched upon in chapter 1, the battle raged with even greater fury during the later Middle Ages.

Towards the latter half of the seventh century, the papacy under Agatho (678–682) defiantly claimed magisterial primacy. At the Easter Synod in Rome the emperor was told in unambiguous terms that the Roman church was his mother and that it had never erred. Incidentally, on this score, the Sixth General Council held a few months later in November 680 condemned Pope Honorius I (625–638) as a heretic for his views in the monothelitic controversy. The conflict continued between Pope Sergius I (687–689) and the Emperor Justinian II (685–712). In 692, Justinian convoked a council without consulting or even inviting Pope Sergius I. He required the pope to sign the decrees of the council and when the pope refused he threatened him with the same fate as Pope Martin I. Two of the pope's trusted advisers were arrested, but the execution of the imperial warrant against the pope himself could not be carried out because of the anger of the Roman populace. The gulf between East and West was widening and gradually, while there may have been little further ideological development, the papacy was beginning to extricate itself from the imperial framework. The letters of Pope Gregory II (715–731) make it very plain that the papacy had not been cowed into abject submission. If anything, they espouse elements which depict claims of superiority. 'We derive our power and authority from the prince of the apostles, Peter, and we could, if we wished, pronounce judgement upon you, but you have already pronounced judgement on yourself and on your counsellors; and you and they may just as well remain accursed.'[13]

It would be false to imagine that the papacy came out of the power struggle of these two centuries as an uncontested victor. But there is little doubt that the position of Bishop of Rome increased in power and stature. It was the pope who on Christmas Day 800, conferred the title of Roman Emperor upon Charlemagne and solemnly crowned him at Rome. By implication, it was the Roman church that created, through the pope, a Christian ruler who was to be the protector and defender of the Christian world. Consider also the coronation of Louis the Pious (814–840) by Pope Stephen IV (816–817) at Rheims in 816. Read the prayer said by Stephen after the blessing of the crown: 'O Christ, Ruler of the empire of the world and Master of the ages, you have willed that Rome be the head of the earthly globe, grant our prayers . . .'[14] At their first meeting it was Louis who prostrated himself three times before the pope. The coronations by the popes of Louis II in 850 and of Charles the Bald in 875 were in the same tradition and served to provide increased prestige to papal power. The latter was presented with the crown 'through the privilege of the apostolic see'.[15] It was during this period that three great influential forgeries saw the light of day. All three — the *Capitula*

Angilramni, Pseudo-Isidore, and *Benedictus Levita* — attempt to give the papal prerogatives the support of antiquity.

In the ninth century, Nicholas I (858—867) with all the ideological arguments of his predecessors, added by *Pseudo-Isidore,* was able to state the case for the plenitude of papal power more forcefully and comprehensively than any of his predecessors. He had the added advantage of the fruitful co-operation of Anastasius, a great librarian and church historian. The learned scholar hailed Nicholas as the 'vicar of God', the 'pontiff of universal mankind', the *'unicus papa'* (one and only pope) and also the 'doorkeeper of heaven'.[16] Adrian II (867—872?) did not take second place to Nicholas in his views and in the exercise of the papal office. He functioned as the vicar of Peter and claimed to inherit all his power. He considered himself to be the supreme monarch within the *societas fidelium* (faithful society), that is, over the corpus of Christendom. The successor to Adrian was John VIII (872—882). For John, the Roman church had supreme jurisdiction over all the nations of the world. Disobedience to his commands was the equivalent of disobedience to divine commands.[17] His main contribution to the theoretical development of papal views of power was that society formed one body corporate and politic; it was headed by him, and it was to be ruled through the instrumentality of the priesthood.

During the tenth century the papacy sank to depths of degradation unparalleled up to that time. Edward Gibbon accused Protestants of dwelling 'with malicious pleasure' upon the scandals of the period.[18] His charge might be well founded, but the judgement appears to be lopsided. More to the point, if 'antichrists' (Gibbon's word) were running the Curia, what then became of the Petrine theory and the doctrine of apostolic succession? Not only Protestant historians, but others without a religious axe to grind have referred to this whole phase in papal history as the 'pornocracy'. Be this as it may, in the pursuit of tracing the development of papal power, it seems unnecessary to dwell, with or without 'malicious pleasure', one moment longer on this period.

Besides, notions of power could hardly be expected to undergo constructive development during such times. This is not the case, however, in the course of the following three centuries. Moving in that direction, the space-time continuum witnessed events which produced even greater advances in the exercise of papal power.

From the accession of Leo IX in 1049 to the death of Boniface VIII in 1303, the papacy exercised, as far as extent and duration were concerned, its greatest degree of supremacy over European society. The tenth century and the first half of the eleventh century had witnessed the increase of imperial domination, which reached its climax under the Emperor Henry III (1046—1056). He was perhaps the most powerful of the early medieval German king-emperors. It was he, with some show of election, that actually appointed Leo IX to the papal throne (1049). Nevertheless, under Leo, a reform movement received impetus that followed a more centralized direction. He presided personally at councils, he took an active part in deposing unworthy prelates, in stringently penalizing simony, in insisting upon clerical celibacy and in attempting to prevent lay interference in clerical elections. His actions were destined to revive the perennial problem of the power struggle in papal-imperial relations. Shortly after his death, the Lateran council of 1059 dictated the famous decree on papal elections. Henceforth, popes were to be chosen by the cardinal bishops of Rome, their choice to be confirmed by the cardinal priests and deacons and acclaimed by the populace. Leo's example, and the determination to follow him, introduced a new chapter into papal history.

Among the associates brought to Rome by Leo was the monk Hildebrand, the future Gregory VII. There was no disagreement between them over the need for reform, and the role of the pope in the affairs of Christendom. If anything, Gregory intensified the papal claims by his views of papal authority. The most outstanding example of such views is found in a series of aphorisms called the *Dictatus Papae.* Some doubt has been raised over the authorship of these statements, but more than likely they are from Gregory himself. The quotation is somewhat lengthy, but it is too noteworthy to run the risk of missing something by attempting a condensed summary.

'The Roman church was founded by God alone.

The Roman bishop is properly called universal.

He alone may depose bishops and reinstate them.

His legate, though of inferior grade, takes precedence in a council of all bishops and may render a decision of deposition against them.

He alone may use the insignia of empire (on basis of *Donation of Constantine*).

The pope is the only person whose feet are kissed by all princes.

His title is unique in the world. [This is the first distinct assertion of the exclusive right of the Bishop of Rome to the title of Pope, once applied to all bishops.]

He may depose emperors.

No council may be regarded as a general one without his consent.

No book or chapter may be regarded as canonical without his authority.

A decree of his may be annulled by no one; he alone may annul the decrees of all.

He may be judged by no one.

No one shall dare to condemn one who appeals to the papal see.

The Roman church has never erred, or ever, by the witness of Scripture, shall err to all eternity.

He may not be considered Catholic who does not agree with the Roman church.

The pope may absolve the subjects of the unjust from their allegiance.'[19]

With the enunciation of such clear-cut concepts of the papal prerogatives, it is not difficult to see how the pontificate of Gregory VII led the papacy towards the establishment of a more centralized ecclesiastical institution. There were introduced a number of practical measures which brought the structure of the church more closely in line with the feudal organization of the states. Legates were used to keep the papacy in better contact with local affairs. Provincial allegiances were broken down by requiring metropolitans to come to Rome for the pallium in person. Bishops were beginning to take an oath of fealty to Rome. Such was Gregory's power and prestige at this time that he did not shrink from deposing the Emperor Henry IV in 1076. What student of history has not heard of the humiliation of Henry at Canossa?

About one hundred years after Gregory VII, the papal throne was occupied by a man who must rank among the greatest of medieval popes, Innocent III (1198–1216). The work of Innocent embraced a greater degree of systematization of theocratic doctrine associated with papal claims than had hitherto been seen. He was able to a very large extent to implement the claims to ultimate and universal authority, which in certain respects had been the ideals for his predecessors. It was during his time that the theory of the two swords took definite root in Western Christendom. Bernard of Clairvaux (1090?–1153), expressed the theory as follows: 'The two swords belong to St Peter. One, the spiritual sword, is in his hands; the other, the temporal sword, is at his command whenever it is necessary to draw it. Peter in fact was told, regarding the sword which seemed the least appropriate to him, "Put thy sword back into its sheath" (John 18:11). It was not for him, therefore, to use it with his own hands.'[20]

The theory of the two swords, the one temporal, the other spiritual, was based upon the Gospel of Luke 22:38: 'And they said, Lord, behold here are two swords. And he said unto them, It is enough.' According to Brian Tierney, 'A whole inverted pyramid of political fantasy was erected on the basis of this one verse of Scripture.'[21] Both swords were at the disposal and under the authority of the papacy. In the letter *Sicut Universitatis Conditor* (1198), Innocent clearly differentiates between the spiritual and secular powers, leaving no doubt that the spiritual is supreme. He uses the analogy of the sun and the moon: the former represented the pontifical authority and the latter the royal.[22] In the decretal *Venerabilem Fratrem* (1202), the argument for the temporal power being subservient to the spiritual rests upon the claim that the very 'right and power' of the emperor comes from the apostolic see. Innocent's assertion is historically rooted in the coronation of Charlemagne by the pope.[23] In one of his sermons on the meaning of pontifical consecration, Innocent declared, 'I have obtained from Peter the mitre for my priesthood and the crown for my royalty; he has made me vicar of Him upon whose vesture is written, King of kings and Lord of lords . . .'[24] In theory, the hegemony of the Bishop of Rome knew no bounds. To him had been given not only 'authority over all the churches' but also 'of the whole world'.[25] During the pontificate of Innocent III nearly every European ruler submitted to the power and authority of the Roman church.

Such intimate and direct association between the secular and the spiritual concepts of power made any theoretical system of separation difficult to maintain. If in theory the pope, as supreme representative of the church, possessed the right of full power over both church and state, any limitation of papal authority would be extremely difficult to define. Innocent tried to do this in the decretal *Novit Ille* (1204), but whether he succeeded or not is highly debatable.[26] This decretal dealt particularly with the papal plenitude of power and was concerned with removing any charges that the papacy was intent on diminishing the jurisdiction or power of the royal prerogatives. Innocent carefully enunciated the divine origin of his office and clearly established the claim that there were no bounds to his ecclesiastical powers with respect to persons. The only limitation upon his supervision was that the matter in hand must be related to spiritual and moral questions. But was this a clearcut restriction of papal power? If political activity could be conducted outside the framework of moral and spiritual matters, there would be no problem, but if judged necessary, the papacy could find some legitimate spiritual justification for intervention in almost every public event. The one whose title was 'Vicar of Jesus Christ and Successor of the Prince of the Apostles,' who was 'the representative of Him to whom belong the earth and all that it contains and all those who inhabit it,' could hardly conceive of papal power as being anything less than 'super-power' with ultimate authority over both the temporal and the spiritual affairs of mankind.[27]

In case the reader suspects too much hyperbole at this point, it would be well to quote at length from the Bull of Innocent IV (1243—1254), *Eger Cui Levia.*

'Whoever seeks to evade the authority of the vicar of Christ . . . thereby impairs the authority of Christ Himself. The King of kings has established us on earth as His universal representative and has conferred full power on us; by giving to the prince of the apostles and to us the power of binding and loosing on earth not only all men whatsoever, but also all things whatsoever . . . The power of temporal government cannot be exercised outside the church, since there is no power constituted by God outside her . . . They are lacking in perspicacity and incapable of investigating the origin of things who imagine that the apostolic see received from Constantine the sovereignty of the empire, whereas it had it previously, as is known, by nature and potentially. Our Lord Jesus Christ, Son of God, true man and true God . . . constituted to the benefit of the holy see a monarchy not only pontifical but royal; he committed to the blessed Peter and his successors the reins of the empire both earthly and celestial, as is indicated by the plurality of the keys. Vicar of Christ [the pope] has received the power to exercise his jurisdiction by the one over the earth for temporal things, by the other in heaven for spiritual things.'[28]

Papal power then, by the middle of the thirteenth century, was theoretically without limitation. According to Innocent IV, it was sacrilegious even to question the plenitude of the papal power. When the pontificate of Boniface VIII was inaugurated in 1294, the papacy was at a high-water mark in its pretensions. Boniface attempted to perpetuate the traditional papal claims, but in his day new forces were beginning to appear on the horizon. Nationalism was one such force and Boniface found himself in disastrous conflict with

Philip IV, King of France. It would be beyond the scope of this study to enter into the many details of the conflict. What is relevant is found in the assertions of Boniface with respect to the extent of papal power. Using the figure of the two swords again and emphasizing the divine origin of his power, he declared that the temporal was subservient to the spiritual.

'We are taught by the words of the Gospel that in this church and in its power there are two swords, a spiritual, to wit, and a temporal . . . both are in the power of the church, namely the spiritual and material swords; the one indeed to be wielded for the church, the other by the church; the former by the priest, the latter by the hand of kings and knights, but at the will and sufferance of that priest. For it is necessary that one sword should be under another and that the temporal authority should be subjected to the spiritual . . . Whoever, therefore, resists this power thus ordained by God, resists the ordination of God . . . Consequently we declare, state, define and pronounce that it is altogether necessary to salvation for every human creature to be subject to the Roman pontiff.'[29]

So great was the power of Boniface that when he presented the crown to the German Emperor Albrecht, it was given under the acknowledgement that the empire had been transferred from the Greeks to the Germans by the pope. When he received the German envoys, he is reported to have been seated on a throne, with a crown upon his head and a sword in his hand, and to have exclaimed, 'I, I am the Emperor!'[30] In the bull *Ausculta fili* (1301), Boniface in his complaints against Philip re-echoed the sentiments of Gregory VII and Innocent III: 'God has placed us, unworthy though we be, over kings and kingdoms in order that we shall root out, destroy, disperse, edify and plant in His name and by His doctrine. Do not allow yourselves to think that you have no superior and that you are not subject to the head of the ecclesiastical hierarchy. Whoever thinks this is a madman; whoever supports him in this belief is a heretic.'[31]

But, as already was mentioned, times were changing, and in the fusillade of verbal exchanges between Philip and

Boniface, the claims of supremacy were being tested in the practical affairs of both church and state. Philip went so far as to attempt a plot to seize Boniface at the papal palace in Anagni, and compel him to resign or bring him before a general church council. The plot failed, and Boniface died shortly thereafter.

Compared with the three centuries before Boniface VIII, there can be little doubt that the following centuries, up till the time of Vatican I in 1870, witnessed a slowing down in the theoretical exposition and the practical exercise of papal power. In the words of Alexander Flick, 'The drama of Canossa had at length been followed by the drama of Anagni.'[32] Boniface may have believed that 'it is altogether necessary to salvation for every human creature to be subject to the Roman pontiff', but the King of France did not. During the fourteenth century, the popes became hardly more than puppets of the French kings. Even the papacy itself was moved to Avignon (1309—1378). Following the 'Babylonian captivity', as it came to be called, with the return of the pope to Rome, there was the scandal of the 'great schism' (1378—1417), when two, and sometimes three rival popes claimed to be the rightful successor of Peter.

The fifteenth century brought the challenge of the Conciliar Movement. Men like John Gerson, Chancellor of the University of Paris, held that a general council was representative of the whole church and was superior to the pope. The fathers at the Council of Constance had ordained in 1415 that, 'This holy synod . . . has received immediately from Christ a power to which all persons, of whatever rank or dignity, not excepting the pope himself, are bound to submit in matters concerning the faith.'[33] This was the age when scholars were imbibing the spirit of the Renaissance, and also were challenging the *status quo* with the cry: *'Ad fontes!'* (To the primary sources!) Obedience to such a cry entailed destructive potential for papal claims to power. However, the full explosive force of this new emphasis, especially with regard to the study of the primary documents of Holy Scripture, was not really felt until some one

hundred years later. It was then, under the passionate zeal
of Martin Luther, that the Reformation had its beginning.
Moreover, it was primarily Luther's acceptance of the
authority of Holy Scripture which prompted his eventual
open revolt against papal power.

It could perhaps be argued that if conciliarism had won
the day the Reformation would never have taken place, but
in history there is no place for what might have been. Within
one generation of the Council of Constance, papal claims
were heard again as loud as ever. The primary objective at
Constance was to end the 'great schism'. This could hardly
be done without general acceptance of the overall authority
of the council. In point of fact, the council declared that all
who held any office in the church, including the pope, were
to be obedient to the council under pain of punishment.
'The main point of conciliarism', as Walter Ullman wrote,
'was that power was not located in the papal monarch but
in the church itself as represented by the general council.'[34]
In a sense then, even the pope was to be a servant of the
council. While it can be said that the council was successful
in ending the schism, it by no means settled the question of
where ultimate authority rested. On 18 January 1460, Pope
Pius II (1458–1464) sounded the death knell of conciliarism
in the papal bull *Execrabilis.*

'A horrible abuse, unheard-of in earlier times, has sprung
up in our period. Some men, imbued with a spirit of rebellion
and moved not by a desire for sound decisions but rather by
a desire to escape the punishment for sin, suppose that they
can appeal from the pope, Vicar of Jesus Christ; from the
pope, to whom in the person of the blessed Peter it was said,
"Feed my sheep", and "Whatever you bind on earth will be
bound in heaven" – from this pope to a future council . . .
we condemn appeals of this kind, reject them as erroneous
and abominable, and declare them to be completely null and
void . . . we lay down that from now on, no one should dare,
regardless of his pretext, to make such an appeal from our
decisions . . . from any commands at all from us or our
successors . . .

'But if anyone — regardless of his status, rank, order or condition, even if he be distinguished by imperial, regal or pontifical dignity — should violate this command when two months have expired from the day this bull has been published in the papal chancery, he by this fact alone incurs excommunication from which he cannot be absolved except through the pope and at the time of death.'[35]

On 21 August 1461, Pius II used *Execrabilis* in a bull of deposition promulgated against Archbishop Diether von Isenburg of Mainz. Pius II was well aware that the German church, universities and courts were by and large strong supporters of conciliarism. Such a bias remained fairly constant right up to the days of Luther. At the Diet of Worms in 1521, a group of German princes supported Luther in his appeal to a council, specifically mentioning Pius II as being out of order in his prohibitions against future councils. Pius II's conflict with Archbishop Diether brought the curialist and conciliarist forces out into the open. Diether had been refused the conferral of the archi-episcopal pallium until he did three things: (1) come to the pope in person for the confirmation; (2) give consent to a crusade tithe upon all income of the German church; and (3) promise never to seek a general council, or assemble the German electors or suffragan bishops without papal permission. Not being daunted, Diether continued to appeal to a future council. This brought about his excommunication.

During the dispute an important tract appeared in defence of the papal position. It was by Gabriel Biel (1425?–1495), a theologian of no mean reputation, and one with whom Luther was well acquainted, as the next chapter will show. Biel's tract is divided into two parts: the first containing nine theses all of which argue dogmatically for the Petrine theory of papal power, and the second setting forth twelve propositions dealing with the deposition of Diether. In the first part, Biel's reasoning moves back and forth over the single theme of St Peter and his successors ruling the church. His purpose in associating St Peter, the apostolic see and the Roman church is to argue for complete obedience to papal authority.[36] 'How could Christ have provided sufficiently for His church', Biel asked, 'if He had not perpetuated in the church the authority granted to Peter to rule it?'[37] A more startling claim in this connection is the contention of Biel that the doctrinal definitions of the church 'must be believed with the same reverence as though it were stated in Holy Scripture'.[38]

Biel's defence of the papal prerogatives was apparently sent to Pius II and was approved by him.[39] There could have been little doubt that approval would be registered for Pius II shared the same sentiments concerning papal authority. In an encyclical which he issued in support of his own candidate for the archbishopric of Mainz he declared, 'Since all kings and rulers of Christendom are accustomed to lend obedience and reverence to the Roman pontiff as the pastor and head of the Christian religion, it is only fitting that they lend support and assistance freely to this pontiff . . . against thieves and robbers, even against the impudence of the wicked who, despising the keys of the church and striving to enter the fold over the wall and not through the gate, usurp with force the rule of metropolitan churches against the will of the pontiff.'[40]

This encyclical began with the Gregorian superscription from the 'servant of the servants of God', and ended with a promise of eternal life to all who would help the apostolic see in its endeavour to overthrow Diether, and who would lend their support to the installation of the papal candidate. That Pius II could make such a promise was based upon the claim, as he himself stated in a later bull issued in 1463, that there was no salvation outside of 'the one catholic and apostolic church'. Also stated very dogmatically was the claim that there could be no approved council without papal authority. How Pius II would have solved the 'great schism' defies explanation. For him, all power flowed from the head to the members. This of course was only 'when there was an unquestioned Roman pontiff'.[41] Since he was 'unquestioned' pope, conciliarism was a moribund matter. One of his successors, Pope Sixtus IV (1471—1484), made so bold as to proclaim that 'The authority to will or not to will a council is fixed solely in the Roman pontiff.'[42] In a war between Sixtus IV and Venice, the Venetians appealed to a general council. The appeal was posted on the doors of St Peter's, Sant'Angelo, and the Pantheon in Rome. The pope responded on 15 July 1483 (the same year as Luther's birth) with *Qui monitis* pronouncing the appeal as being null and void, sacrilegious and detestable, and excommunicated the Doge of Venice and his supporters.

Papal opposition to conciliarism continued unabated into the next century. In July 1509, Pope Julius II (1503–1513) promulgated *Suscepti regiminis,* in which he insisted that *Execrabilis* was of enduring validity; exclaiming also that anyone appealing to a future council would be considered as a schismatic. Luther's challenge was only one decade away. Papal attitudes were adamantly fixed. How could any change be expected? The impasse was illustrated by the bull *Exsurge Domine* which was issued on 15 June 1520. Pope Leo X (1513–1522) was aiming primarily at Luther, but in doing so he drew ammunition directly from *Execrabilis* and from *Suscepti regiminis.* He likened Luther to a wild boar which had entered the sacred vineyard of the church. Whether the image came from Leo X's immediate setting, for at the time of the issuance of this bull he was at his lodge hunting wild boar, or from Holy Scripture (Psalm 80:13; Acts 8:3) is a moot question. Leo X listed forty-one of Luther's supposed errors. Numbers twenty-five to twenty-nine dealt with the attack upon papal claims. According to inside information which Luther received in October 1519 from a former fellow-student, Crotus Rubianus, then in Italy, the thing which angered the papal court more than anything else about Luther was his appeal for a general council.[43] Such appeals were viewed as open attacks upon papal power. However, the capstone in Luther's revolt took place at 9 a.m. on 10 December 1520. On this morning, Luther dramatically flung *Exsurge Domine* on the top of a fire already burning with volumes of the canon law, the papal decretals and scholastic philosophy. The action was the climax of a three-year struggle, which had begun with the indulgence controversy back in 1517. It was a symbolical act which had momentous consequences as far as the future extent of papal power was concerned, and even the future course of European history. This study could hardly be complete without giving some consideration to what it was that brought about Luther's revolt.

NOTES

[1] E. Giles, *Documents Illustrating Papal Authority A.D. 96–454* (London: S.P.C.K., 1952), xvii.
[2] The episcopate of Clement is not without difficulties. See *The Apostolic Fathers*, Part I (London: Griffith Farran Okeden and Welsh, n.d.), p.151.
[3] For the Roman Catholic view see: Thomas S. Dolan, *The See of Peter and the Voice of Antiquity* (St Louis: B. Herder, 1908).
[4] Cyril C. Richardson, in his introduction to *Clement's First Letter* makes a number of observations worth noting. (1) There is no evidence that Corinth applied to Rome for a judgement. (2) It was nothing extraordinary for leaders of one church to send a letter of advice and warning to another congregation. The apostolic practice set a precedent which was followed by Ignatius, by Polycarp, by Dionysius of Corinth, by Serapion and by many others. (3) Each Christian community seems to have felt a sense of responsibility for the others. Local churches were not conceived as being totally isolated and autonomous units. (4) This document was written in the name of the congregation. (5) It is very far from a papal decree and makes no claim to superior authority. (6) Basing its admonitions on the authority of Scripture, it exercises persuasion to attain its objective. Cyril C. Richardson (trans. & ed.), *Early Christian Fathers* (Philadelphia, The Westminster Press), p. 35.
[5] J. B. Lightfoot, *The Apostolic Fathers* (MacMillan, 1889), vol. II, p. 558.
[6] Dr Kidd, *Documents Illustrative of the History of the Church,* vol. I, No. 74 (S.P.C.K.), p. 124.
[7] John Schulte, *Roman Catholicism, Old and New, from the Standpoint of the Infallibility Doctrine* (Toronto: Belford Brothers, 1876), p. 245.
[8] C. F. Rogers, *Rome and the Early Church* (London: S.P.C.K.), pp. 17–19.
[9] Walter Ullman, *A Short History of the Papacy in the Middle Ages* (London: Methuen & Co. Ltd., 1972), p. 6.
[10] C. F. Rogers, *op. cit.,* p. 25.
[11] Walter Ullman, *op. cit.,* p. 39.
[12] Ullmann, *The Growth of Papal Government in the Middle Ages* (New York: Books for Libraries Press, Inc., 1967), p. 28.
[13] *Ibid.,* p. 46.
[14] *Ibid.,* p. 145.
[15] *Ibid.,* p. 161.
[16] *Ibid.,* p. 192.
[17] *Ibid.,* p. 220.

[18] Edward Gibbon, *The History of the Decline and Fall of the Roman Empire* (London: Ward, Lock and Co. N.D.), vol. II, p. 406.
[19] Joseph H. Dahmus, *A History of Medieval Civilization* (New York: The Odyssey Press, 1964), pp. 525, 526.
[20] Wladimir D'Ormesson, *The Papacy*, pp. 63–64.
[21] Brian Tierney, *The Crisis of Church and State* (New Jersey: Prentice-Hall, Inc., 1964), p. 8.
[22] 'Just as God, founder of the universe, has constituted two large luminaries in the firmament of heaven, a major one to dominate the day and a minor one to dominate the night, so he has established in the firmament of the universal church, which is signified by the name of heaven, two great dignities, a major one to preside, so to speak, over the days of the souls, and a minor one to preside over the nights of the bodies. They are the pontifical authority and the royal power. Thus, as the moon receives its light from the sun and for this very reason is minor both in quantity and in quality, in its size and in its effect, so the royal power derives from the pontifical authority the splendour of its dignity, the more of which is inherent in it, the less is the light with which it is adorned, whereas the more it is distant from its reach.' *Readings in Church History*, ed. Colman J. Barry, vol. I, (2 vols, Westminster, Maryland, The Newman Press, 1960), pp. 438–439.
[23] 'Just as we – who owe justice to particular persons according to the service connected with the apostolic office – do not want our justice to be usurped by others, so we do not wish to vindicate to ourselves the rights of the princes. Wherefore we recognize, as we should, the right and power of those princes to whom it is known to pertain by right and ancient custom to elect a king who is subsequently to be promoted to the dignity of emperor; and particularly so as this right and power has come to them from the apostolic see, which had transferred the Roman Empire from the Greeks to the Germans in the person of Charlemagne. But, on the other hand, the princes should recognize, and they actually do recognize, that the right and authority to examine the person elected as king – who is to be promoted to the office emperor – belongs to us, who anoint, consecrate and crown him. For it is usually and generally observed that the examination of the person appertains to him to whom belongs the laying-on of hands. Consequently, if the princes not only be divided votes but even unanimously elected as king a sacrilegious or excommunicated man, a tyrant or an idiot, a heretic or a pagan, should we anoint, consecrate and crown such a man? Certainly not!' *Ibid.*, pp. 437–438.
[24] C. S. M. Walker, *The Gathering Storm* (Grand Rapids: Wm. B. Eerdmans Company, 1961), p. 164.
[25] *Ibid.*, pp. 163–164.
[26] *Readings in Church History*, vol. I, pp. 436–437.
[27] Wladimir D'Ormesson, *op. cit.*, p. 62.
[28] Bernard Guillemain, *The Later Middle Ages*, trans. S. Taylor, vol. 77 of the *Twentieth Century Encyclopedia of Catholicism*, ed. Henri Daniel-Rops (New York: Hawthorne Books, 1959), pp. 37–38.
[29] *Readings in Church History*, vol. I, pp. 466–467.

The more important formulae of *Unam Sanctam* has been summarized by Henri Daniel-Rops:

'(1) There is only one church, outside which there is no salvation. (2) The church has only one Head, Christ, who has delegated His authority to His vicar, the successor of St Peter. (3) The pope has two swords, one spiritual, the other temporal; the first is wielded by the church, i.e., by the pope, for the good of souls, the second is entrusted to kings, who may not use it except in the higher interests of Christianity and under the pope's direction. (4) The temporal is subject to the spiritual, which may pass judgement upon it if it goes astray. Consequently, (5) No one can be saved unless he willingly submits to the pope.' Henri Daniel-Rops, *Cathedral and Crusade* (London: J. M. Dent and Sons, Ltd., 1957), p. 570.

[30] Alexander Clarence Flick, *The Decline of the Medieval Church* (2 vols.; New York: Alfred A. Knopp, 1930), vol. I, 17.

[31] *Ibid.*, p. 25.

[32] *Ibid.*, p. 30.

[33] Geddes MacGregor, *The Vatican Revolution* (London: MacMillan & Co. Ltd., 1958), p. 40.

[34] Ullman, *A Short History of the Papacy*, p. 299.

[35] Heiko A. Oberman, Daniel E. Zerfoss, and William J. Courtenay, trans., and ed., *Defensorium Obedientiae Apostolicae Et Alia Documenta* (Cambridge: The Belknap Press of Harvard University, 1968), pp. 225, 227.

[36] *Ibid.*, pp. 85—87.

[37] *Ibid.*, p. 91.

[38] *Ibid.*, p. 75.

[39] *Ibid.*, p. 58.

[40] *Ibid.*, pp. 349—355.

[41] *Ibid.*, pp. 357—365.

[42] *Ibid.*, p. 5.

[43] James Atkinson, *The Trial of Luther* (London: B. T. Batsford Ltd., 1971), p. 80.

3
Luther's revolt against papal power

Luther's affixing of the *Ninety-Five Theses* near the entrance
of the Castle Church at Wittenberg on 31 October 1517 was
not in itself intended as an attack upon papal authority. In
reality, as one author has pointed out, the event 'had no
more significance for his contemporaries than the positing
of a subject for discussion by the Oxford Union would have
today'.[1] However, even though Luther did not consider his
action as being indicative of disloyalty to any of his ecclesiastical superiors, it did thrust him into the limelight of public
controversy, which in turn, led to his open revolt against the
papal institution.

Throughout 1518, there was no apparent indication that
Luther had any avowed intention of formally breaking with
the Roman church. His testimony before Cardinal Cajetan,
the papal legate to the Diet at Augsburg, in October, bore
this out. His words were as follows: 'Above all, I, brother
Martin Luther, Augustinian, declare publicly that I cherish
and follow the holy Roman church in all my words and
actions — present, past and future.'[2] He was able to make
this declaration even though certain doubts were beginning
to arise concerning the papal system and the extent of its
authority over the life and doctrine of the church. These
doubts were briefly mentioned in his *Explanations of the
Ninety-Five Theses* published the month prior to his hearing
at Augsburg. But even this must not be interpreted to mean
that he was consciously beginning an attack on the pope or
on the papal office. In October 1518, he spoke of the pope
as 'the Most Holy Lord our Pope . . .'[3] A few months later,

in January 1519, he wrote a letter to the pope and addressed him as 'Your Holiness and August Majesty'.[4] In this same letter he wrote, 'I was deeply grieved that my most loyal service has had such an unhappy outcome and that what I had undertaken — to guard the honour of the Roman church — had resulted in disgrace and was suspected of all wickedness, even so far as the head of the church was concerned.'[5]

In spite of the fact that he had already met with official ecclesiastical opposition in 1518, both at Heidelberg in May, and at Augsburg in October, Luther still considered himself to be completely orthodox. The contrast, however, between what he said at the beginning of 1519 and what he said by the end of 1520 about the papacy and the Roman church is truly amazing. By the middle of 1520, he was able without any mitigation to identify the papacy with the Antichrist of Holy Scripture and to declare without any reservation that the true church of God had nothing whatever to do with it. What brought about the change? In the preface of his *Lectures on Galatians,* published shortly after the Leipzig Disputation, he traced the beginning of the turning-point to the days when he 'babbled forth some trifling observations about indulgences'.[6]

The intention of Luther in posting the *Ninety-Five Theses* and the indirect consequences of his intention must therefore be distinguished. His primary intention was born 'out of love and zeal for truth and the desire to bring it to light'.[7] He seemed to be possessed of a naive confidence which led him to believe that all he needed to do was to turn the light of truth on and the darkness of error would vanish of its own accord. His opposition was directed towards what he termed 'impious, false and heretical'[8] teachings which were associated with the granting of indulgences.

Luther, besides being a professor at Wittenberg, was a pastor, and part of the motivation for his becoming involved in the indulgence controversy came from deep pastoral concern. His heart, as well as his head, was involved. He wanted to see truth prevail, not merely to satisfy some

intellectual ambition, but more directly because he believed
that the propagation of error had eternal consequences for
his flock. Luther's position on these points could hardly
be intended as a direct attack on the authority of the papacy.
If it had been understood by his contemporaries as such,
Erasmus would hardly have declared that Luther's views
were approved by the best men and that the *Ninety-Five
Theses* had received a universal welcome.

In spite of Luther's immediate intentions in writing the
Ninety-Five Theses, within approximately three years of
their publication his formal break with the Roman Catholic
Church was a fact. His own testimony, as far as what
prompted him to challenge the misuse of indulgences, was
his emphasis upon the authority of Holy Scripture. He wrote
that he was 'measuring sins and errors by the standard of
God's commandments and the most holy gospel of Christ'.[9]
This point was of fundamental importance, for while some
modern Roman Catholic scholars recognize that the particular indulgence in question 'was being misused by the Curia
and the Archbishop of Mainz'[10] and was a 'classic example
of scandal',[11] it obviously involved much more for Luther.
Consider, for example, what he wrote in theses 32 and 62:

'32. Those who believe that they can be certain of their
salvation because they have indulgence letters will be eter-
nally damned, together with their teachers.

62. The true treasure of the church is the most holy
gospel of the glory and grace of God.'[12]

Even a cursory reading of the theses reveals that the main
issue was not primarily a matter of financial exploitation.
Very clearly, Luther was concerned over the doctrinal
aberrations that he believed were present in the instructions
and the sermons associated with the sale of the indulgence
letters. He felt that they were the cause of much gross
misunderstanding among the people. For example, the
Dominican John Tetzel, one of the preachers entrusted with
the promotion of the indulgences, purportedly preached that
through confession, penance and the placing of 'alms into
the coffer', a plenary indulgence could be obtained which

could apply both to the 'complete remission' of all sins and to the redemption of dead parents and others who suffer in purgatory.[13] A contemporary chronicler wrote that Tetzel claimed 'that even if someone had slept with Christ's dear mother, the pope had power in heaven and on earth to forgive as long as money was put into the indulgence coffer'.[14] Luther, in thesis 75, appeared to support this report. However, Tetzel denied having made such a claim.

In a letter written to the Archbishop of Mainz on the same day that he posted the *Ninety-Five Theses,* Luther wrote more specifically about the confusion caused by the sale of indulgences. He manifested much concern about the false assurance of salvation that accompanied the buying of indulgences. He also challenged the teaching 'that souls escape from purgatory as soon as they have placed a contribution in the chest'.[15] In a more sweeping statement he declared that, 'Indulgences contribute absolutely nothing to the salvation and holiness of souls . . .'[16] In his estimation, 'The first and only duty of the bishops . . . is to see that the people learn the gospel and the love of Christ.'[17] His reason for so bold a statement was found in the fact that Christ never 'ordered that indulgences should be preached, but he forcefully commanded the gospel to be preached'.[18]

Things began to move very rapidly after the *Ninety-Five Theses* obtained a wide circulation. The invention of the printing press proved fateful. Apparently, Luther's original intention was to keep the theses for scholarly consideration alone, but to his consternation they were translated into German and made available to a wider audience. On 5 March 1518, he wrote, 'I merely intended to submit them to a few learned men for examination, and if they approved of them, to suppress them.'[19] Reactions to the theses were somewhat contradictory. On the surface there was nothing in them that appeared revolutionary. Men like Sylvester Prierias (1456?–1523), a Dominican theologian and adviser to Pope Leo X, were able to study them and to conclude that Luther was guilty of heresy, while other men, like Cardinal Cajetan (1469–1534), the general of the Dominican order and a man reputed to have been 'the greatest theologian of his time',[20] concluded that they furnished no substantial ground for a charge of heresy. The problem, therefore, was not so much in what Luther actually said, but in what his statements implied.

Within a matter of weeks the theses were circulated throughout the whole of Germany.[21] They had an adverse effect upon the indulgence traffic. Tetzel retaliated by attacking Luther, called him a heretic and boasted that within three weeks Luther would be in flames. The controversy was quick to elicit the attention of other theologians. In January 1518, Johann Eck (1486—1543), Professor of Theology at the University of Ingolstadt in Bavaria, published his *Obelisks*,[22] in which he asserted that Luther's views were similar to those of John Huss, who had been burned as a heretic in 1415. By this time the papacy had been informed of the disturbance in Germany. At first, Pope Leo X interpreted the trouble as a monkish quarrel, and did not take the matter seriously. However, in February 1518, Leo X directed the Pro-magistrate of the Augustinian Order, Gabriel della Volta, to send instructions to Staupitz 'to quiet the man'. The matter was brought before the general chapter of the Order held at Heidelberg during April and May. There appears to be little specific information as to what official action was taken against Luther.

During these early months of 1518, it already seemed apparent to some observers that inherent in Luther's views were some implications which challenged the power of the papacy. When the Archbishop of Mainz received Luther's theses, he turned to the theological faculty of the University of Mainz for their expert opinion. After careful examination, they decided to put the whole matter before the authority of the Roman Curia. Among other things, they noted that the theses limited 'the power of the pope and the apostolic see . . .'[23] Luther had written to the Bishop of Brandenburg a letter similar to the one received by the Archbishop of Mainz. The answer, probably written on 13 February 1518, clearly pointed out that Luther was attacking the authority of the church.[24] Johann Eck was of the same opinion. Luther knew this, for in a letter that he wrote on 24 March 1518, he said, 'In his *Obelisks,* he [Eck] calls me a fanatic Hussite, heretical, seditious, insolent and rash, not to speak of such slight abuse as that I am dreaming, clumsy, unlearned and that I despise the pope.'[25] There were others outside the church who also detected a note of rebellion against papal power. On 3 April 1518, Ulrich von Hutten (1488–1523) wrote to a friend, 'Maybe you have not heard. A faction at Wittenberg in Saxony has risen in insurrection against the sovereign pontiff: another is assuming the defence of the papal indulgences.'[26]

As far as the indulgence controversy itself was concerned, Luther's interpretation of the 'treasury of the church' was modified by an evangelical emphasis which he drew from Holy Scripture. It was this emphasis which led him to conclude that 'The saints have no superabundant merits . . .'[27] and that 'The merits of Christ are so to speak a treasury, not of the church, but of God the Father, for through His efficacious intercession before God Christ obtained for us remission of guilt.'[28] These sentiments possessed, as far as Luther's opponents were concerned, some disturbing ecclesiological implications. By reinterpreting the doctrine of the treasury in the light of Holy Scripture, he dissociated the question of the doctrine of salvation from the framework of the authority of the Roman ecclesiastical institution.

Luther's opponents seemed to have apprehended the seriousness of this matter before Luther did himself. Sylvester Prierias, the one commissioned by Pope Leo X to refute Luther, brought the issue into sharp focus when he asserted that, 'The universal church is virtually the Roman church which consists representatively in the cardinals, but virtually in the pope. Just as the universal church cannot err on faith and morals, nor can a true council, neither can the Roman church nor the pope when speaking in his official capacity. Whoever does not accept the doctrine of the Roman church and of the Roman pontiff as the infallible rule of faith, from which the sacred Scripture derives strength and authority, is a heretic. And he who declares that in the matter of indulgences the Roman church cannot do what it actually does is a heretic.'[29]

During the Diet at Augsburg in the fall of 1518, the question of authority began to assume a more prominent place in the controversy. In August, Luther had received a citation to come to Rome within sixty days to answer the accusations of heresy. Through the influence of his ruler, Frederick the Wise, this summons was changed, and Luther was to be examined before Cardinal Cajetan at Augsburg. The encounter took place in October, but it proved fruitless. Luther's account of the meeting appeared on 25 November under the title *Proceedings at Augsburg*. According to Luther, the difference between himself and Cajetan was evident. Like Prierias, Cajetan rested his case on the authority of the pope. For Luther the authority was Holy Scripture. At the first meeting Luther was requested to recant. He replied by asking to be shown wherein he had erred. Two of his theses were declared to be contrary to Catholic doctrine. The first was the fifty-eighth of the *Ninety-Five Theses*, which declared that 'the treasures of the church' were not identical with 'the merits of Christ',[30] and the second was a sentence in the seventh thesis of the *Explanations* which stated that it was not the sacrament of penance, but faith that justified a man.[31] The meaning of the word 'treasure' in the bull *Unigenitus* was also a source of contention.

Luther did not hesitate to declare that *Unigenitus* was a document characterized by verbosity and stuffed with ignorance.[32] His main criticism was based primarily on the way that *Unigenitus* 'distorts the Holy Scriptures and audaciously twists the words into a meaning which they do not have in their context, in fact into a contrary meaning'.[33] Luther declared that the one thing he sought in the hearing before Cajetan was 'the true meaning of Scripture'.[34] With such a canon to guide him, he found it possible to question the traditional papal interpretation of Matthew 16:18, 19. His emphasis upon the authority of Scripture led him also to take issue with those teachers who 'fix the church of Christ in time and place'.[35] He went on to declare that one can be a Christian without being in submission to the pope. He traced the title of universal bishop, which belonged to the pope, back to the time of St Gregory (590—604).[36] And he viewed the power of the pope, not so much as existing by divine right, but in terms of Romans 13:1, that is, as one of the powers that be. In other words, it was to be supported and honoured in the same sense as was the secular power.[37]

Immediately after the encounter at Augsburg, Cajetan sought from Rome a less ambiguous statement about indulgences. This prompted the composition of the papal bull *Cum Postquam* (9 November 1518). The content of the bull carefully pointed out both the primacy of the Roman church and that of the Roman pontiff. As the vicar of Jesus Christ on earth, the pope had 'the power of the keys, to which it belongs to open the kingdom of heaven, by removing the obstacles in the faithful in Christ . . .'[38] By virtue of his apostolic authority, the pope could 'concede indulgences from the superabundant merits of Christ and the saints to these same faithful of Christ . . . whether they be in this life or in purgatory . . .'.[39] The indulgence of the church was to be 'held by all and be preached under punishment of excommunication, of a sentence [automatically] imposed (*latae sententiae*)'.[40]

The contents of *Cum Postquam* placed Luther on the horns of a dilemma. He had already made public his opinion that indulgences belonged to those things which were permitted by the church. They were not meritorious and did not release souls from purgatory. He had been able to say these things because he believed that the church had not settled the question. What could he say now? *Cum Postquam* authoritatively and officially confirmed the arguments of Cajetan. What is more, the doctrine was binding under pain of excommunication. Luther viewed the 'new decretal' as a most unusual document. For one thing, it contained no citations from the Holy Scriptures, canon law or the church fathers. It was, therefore, in his eyes a collection of unsupported claims which he could not acknowledge as being the doctrine of the 'holy church'.[41]

The early months of 1519 proved to be the watershed of Luther's career. Towards the end of January, Luther became entangled once again in controversy with the theologian, Johann Eck. On 29 December 1518, Eck had announced that there would be a disputation between himself and Karlstadt, Luther's colleague and Dean of the Theological Faculty at the University of Wittenberg. It had been agreed by the two theologians that the debate should be held at Leipzig. In preparation for the debate, Eck had published twelve theses which he would defend. Eleven of them dealt with indulgences and the twelfth was concerned with papal supremacy. The twelfth was clearly an attack on Luther's explanation of thesis 72. Luther, in the *Explanations,* had raised some doubts about the jurisdiction of the Roman church over other churches.[42] From what Luther read in Eck's theses, he believed that they were aimed at his own teachings. Therefore, Luther entered the fray and in February published twelve counter-theses. The last of these theses declared that it was doubtful whether the power and the position of the pope could be justified historically. It was evident that this was the main issue, and that the forth-coming disputation would feature Luther, rather than Karlstadt, as Eck's opponent.

Motivated by the renewed encounter with Eck, Luther was obliged to enter into a deeper study of church history and the papal decretals. On 13 March he wrote to Spalatin and made reference to his preparation for the Leipzig dis-putation. After describing the nature of his studies, he confided, 'I do not know whether the pope is the Antichrist himself or whether he is his apostle, so miserable is Christ (that is, the truth) corrupted and crucified by the pope in the decretals.'[43] During the course of the controversy, Eck added another thesis to the original twelve. It was con-cerned with the freedom of the will. This one became thesis 7, and the one on papal authority became thesis 13. Luther's response, his *Disputation and Defence of Brother Martin Luther against the Accusations of Dr Johann Eck* was pub-lished in May. This work became the basis for the debate with Eck at Leipzig in July. At the centre of the debate were the questions concerning the authority of the pope and the jurisdiction of the Roman church. Luther's argument was that the primacy of the Bishop of Rome rested solely upon the papal decrees of the preceding four hundred years.[44] However, more than this, he clearly implied that the authority of the pope was contrary to the teaching of Scripture. He argued that Christ had not singled out Peter to bestow upon him alone a jurisdiction over the other apostles which could be transferred to the successive Roman bishops. He also asserted that both the papacy and church councils were liable to err.[45] Luther's position on the papacy was now out in the open and, as long as he held to it, there could be no hope of reconciliation with the Roman church.

It was two months after Leipzig, on 3 September, that Luther published his lectures on Galatians. Not only did he repeat his conviction 'that the council and the pope had erred and can err',[46] but he apparently realized that his real battle was with the power of the pope and the privileges of the Roman church. About this same time the implications of his emphasis upon the authority of Holy Scripture began to dawn more clearly upon his own thinking. After describing the theological confusion of his day and the lack of a common source of authority, he concluded that 'Necessity itself compels us to flee for refuge to the most solid rock of divine Scripture and not to believe rashly any, whoever they may be, who speak, decide or act contrary to its authority.'[47]

He was not unaware that his views brought him under the threat of excommunication, and if pursued further would lead inexorably to excommunication itself. But, by the end of 1519, he had adopted such a concept of the nature of the church that excommunication was something no longer to be feared. The basic reason for this was that excommunication could exclude only from external membership in the ecclesiastical organization of the church. It could not really separate a man from the true church. To apprehend Luther's feelings on this matter, it is necessary to understand that he had by this time come to conceive of the true church as that 'inner, spiritual and invisible fellowship of the heart, by which one is incorporated by true faith, hope and love in the fellowship of Christ and of all the saints . . .'[48] This fellowship cannot be given or taken away by anyone, 'be he bishop, pope, or angel or any creature'.[49]

In February 1520, Luther found occasion to read Hutten's edition of Valla's exposure of the *Donation of Constantine,* and as a result he wrote, 'I have scarcely doubt that the pope is the Antichrist expected by the world, so closely do their acts, lives, sayings and laws agree.'[50] In the early part of June 1520, he added to this conclusion some words of exceptional vehemence which appear to mark a solemn and a final forging of his feelings towards Rome: 'Farewell, unhappy, hopeless, blasphemous Rome! The wrath of God is come upon thee, as thou deservest . . . We have cared for Babylon, and she is not healed; let us leave her then, that she may be the habitation of dragons, spectres and witches and, true to her name of Babel, an everlasting confusion, a new pantheon of wickedness.'[51]

On 15 June 1520, Leo X signed the bull *Exsurge Domine.* Luther was given sixty days to recant, or else suffer the consequences of excommunication. According to the relationship which then existed between church and state, excommunication would be accompanied by a ban under which Luther would be considered an outlaw. The bull began, 'Arise, O Lord, and judge Thy cause . . . the cause of the holy Roman church, the mother of all churches, and mistress of the faith . . .'[52] On 10 October, or shortly before that date, the bull arrived in Wittenberg. It was sent by Johann Eck, who had been largely responsible for its issuance. The senate of the university refused to put it into effect without having first received the advice and orders of the electoral court. Apparently, the bull was not officially delivered to Luther personally. He had seen it and was aware of its contents, but it seems as though he decided to act as if it had not been legally turned over to him. On 30 October, he wrote to Duke John Frederick, the son of Duke John, the brother and successor of Elector Frederick, 'As the bull has in no way frightened me, I intend to preach, lecture and write in spite of it.'[53] Even as late as 17 November, he appeared to have some doubts whether the bull would be put into effect. This may have been due to the fact that certain bishops, like the one at Bamberg, refused or hesitated to publish and execute the bull in their dioceses. It may also have been due to the prevalence of the idea that the final word on Luther's teaching could only be spoken by a general council.[54]

Exsurge Domine must have arrived in Luther's hands by 10 December, for on that day (sixty days after the bull appeared in Wittenberg), along with volumes of the canon law, the papal decretals and scholastic philosophy, he cast it into the mounting flames of a fire which had been built expressly for such a purpose. This dramatic act of defiance was committed at the eastern gate near the Church of the Holy Cross in Wittenberg. Writing about it approximately one month later, Luther said, 'I have burned the books of the pope and the bull, at first with trembling and praying; but now I am more pleased with this than with any other action of my life, for [these books] are worse than I had thought.'[55] The papal bull had demanded the burning of Luther's books. At the instigation of Eck and the papal nuncio, Jerome Aleander, this had been done at Louvain, Cologne and Mainz.

Before the year 1520 had run its course, Luther wrote the treatise, *Why the Books of the Pope and His Disciples Were Burned.* In this work he declared that the doctrine of the pope and his disciples was 'antichristian, devilish doctrine'.[56] He also, without reservation, identified the pope with the Antichrist of Holy Scripture.

In the early part of 1521, there could be no further question about the break with the Roman church. Luther's excommunication was proclaimed on 3 January 1521, in the bull *Decet Romanum Pontificem.* But it was of no consequence to Luther for, by 1521, his attitude towards the papacy and towards the Roman church had completely

changed. In March 1521 he wrote, 'But I claim that if St
Peter himself were sitting in Rome today I would still deny
that he is pope and supposed to rule over all other bishops
by divine right. The papacy is a human invention of which
God knows nothing. All churches are equal, and their unity
does not depend on the sovereignty of this one man, but as
St Paul says in Ephesians 4, their unity depends on one
faith, one baptism, one Lord Jesus Christ, and these are all
in common and equal possession of all the parishes in the
world.'[57]

Luther's revolt against papal power had led him to
strike at the very heart of papal claims, that is, the Petrine
theory itself. The controversy had started inconspicuously
as an inquiry into the power and efficacy of indulgences.
But since the granting of indulgences was associated with
the power and position of the pope, it was not long before
this became the central issue. When Luther objected to
abuses in the granting of indulgences, it was interpreted by
his opponents as an indication of disloyalty to the pope and
hence, therefore, to the church. In Luther's own eyes this
was not the case. He did not consider himself to be a traitor
to the valid traditions of the church. But he was caught on
the horns of a dilemma. The ecclesiastical authority with
which he controverted claimed to be the visible embodiment
of apostolic tradition. This left him with no alternative but
to re-examine the doctrinal foundations of Roman Catholic
ecclesiology.

In order to appreciate more fully the rationale behind
Luther's opposition to the ecclesiastical authority of the
Roman church and his subsequent emphasis upon the spiritual nature of the church, it would be helpful to gain a
better understanding of the motives which prompted his
concern over the scandalous traffic in indulgences. For
Luther in 1517, the main question was clearly the false
security that was engendered by the hawking of indulgences.
At heart, it was a conflict involving two different systems of
salvation.

According to the main traditions of the Roman church,

man was able by his own native ability to contribute in some way to his own salvation. This was accomplished by the accumulation of merit through the efficacious value of good works. In scholastic theory there were two forms of merit. The first, known as congruent merit, was something which man received by his own application to spiritual concerns. By this process man received the internal grace which then enabled him to perform works of a quality hitherto unattainable. These latter works were classified as condign merit and they were the basis for more grace, and finally led to heavenly glory.

Luther, during his early years in the monastery, was caught up in a distinct stream of merit theology which flowed from an academic-theological system known as nominalism. It had been controversial since the eleventh century and by the fourteenth century had so pervaded the European universities that 'nobody was allowed to ignore it'.[58] An extreme form of nominalism, which was associated with the name of William of Ockham, had triumphed at the University of Erfurt.[59] This was the place where Luther earned his M.A. degree. One of Luther's teachers at Erfurt, Bartholomew Arnoldi von Usingen, was a dedicated disciple of Gabriel Biel (1425?–1495), who was one of the outstanding Ockhamists of the fifteenth century. Not only did Usingen stand close to Biel in time and thought, but he was 'a true disciple of Biel with respect to the doctrine of justification'.[60] There can be little doubt that Luther was familiar with Biel's theology. The text book he read for ordination in 1507 was Biel's treatise on *The Canon of the Mass*. In October 1516 he wrote to John Lang mentioning that he was familiar with Biel, but that he disagreed with him on such matters as grace, charity, hope, faith and virtue, adding, 'He is a Pelagian.'[61]

The significance of associating Luther with the theology of Biel emerges when one begins to understand Biel's doctrine of justification. First of all, it was theologically tied to ecclesiology. Biel could speak of 'justification by grace alone', but only because he had made a rational distinction

between the *potentia absoluta* and the *potentia ordinata* of
God. The former signified the absolute power of God, subject only to the law of non-contradiction; and the latter
referred to the order established by God in which He chose
to act in providing man's salvation. Justification by grace
came within the framework of *potentia absoluta*. Justification by works fell under the *potentia ordinata*, that is,
under the divinely ordained jurisdiction of the ministry of
the church. In practice, it meant that justification was a
process under the supervision of the church. Man was responsible by his own native powers to eschew evil and to
choose good, in order to create the proper disposition for the
reception of grace. Unless man were able by his own power
to do what lay within him, he could not merit the infusion
of grace.[62]

There does not appear to be any substantial evidence to
doubt that Luther was embroiled in this Ockhamist system
of merit theology when he entered the monastery. By his
own native ability he wanted to arrive at a pure love for God.
He believed that if he did this, he could acquire the merit of
congruence. If he thus provided the correct disposition, God
in His mercy could reward him with His grace. Adorned with
grace, he could then perform meritorious works, by virtue of
which he would become worthy to receive eternal life. With
great earnestness he pursued this goal. But he could not
overcome the torments of doubt and fear, the fruit of
repeated self-examination which revealed to him that he was
falling short of the divine standard. He found that his very
nature was infected by sin, which caused him relentless
anxiety of soul. He was determined by strict observance of
his monastic vows to find favour with God. Speaking of his
monastic life, he said, 'I was indeed a pious monk and kept
the rules of my order so strictly that I can say: if ever a monk
gained heaven through monkery, it should have been I.'[63]

The precise time and place when Luther resolved his spiritual problem concerning how God justifies the sinner appears
to be an open question. Suggested dates range all the way
from 1509 to 1519.[64] Luther himself, in his autobiographical

preface to his Latin works written towards the end of his life in 1545, made it clear that he found the answer in St Paul's Epistle to the Romans, chapter 1:17. However, this testimony does not allow for a definite dating of his new understanding of justification.[65] But there is good reason to suppose that he had arrived at his new appreciation of justification by at least 1516.[66] Certainly, by this year he had repudiated the Ockhamist doctrine of justification. In his lectures on Romans, completed in 1516, he declared, 'Wherefore it is mere madness for them to say that a man of his own powers is able to love God above all things and to do the works of the law in substance, if not literally, without grace. Fools! Theologians for swine! According to them grace would not be necessary save for a new requirement above the law. For if the law is fulfilled by our own powers, as the way, then grace would not be necessary for the fulfilment of the law, but only for a new exaction beyond the law. Who can bear these sacrilegious opinions?'[67]

Not only had Luther parted company with the Ockhamist theologians on this point, but he clearly believed that he had arrived at a more accurate understanding of the divine processes of justification. On 8 April 1516, Luther wrote in a letter to George Spenlein, an Augustinian friar in the monastery at Wittenberg: 'Now I should like to know whether your soul, tired of its own righteousness, is learning to be revived by and to trust in the righteousness of Christ. For in our age the temptation to presumption besets many, especially those who try with all their might to be just and good without knowing the righteousness of God, which is most bountifully and freely given us in Christ. They try to do good of themselves in order that they might stand before God clothed in their own virtues and merits. But this is impossible . . . Therefore, my dear friar, learn Christ and Him crucified. Learn to praise Him, and despairing of yourself, say, "Lord Jesus, You are my righteousness, just as I am Your sin. You have taken upon Yourself what is mine and have given to me what is Yours. You have taken upon Yourself what You were not and have given to me what I was not" . . . For why was it necessary for Him to die if we can obtain a good conscience by our own works and afflictions? Accordingly you will find peace only in Him and only when you despair of yourself and your own works. Besides, you will learn from Him that just as He has received you, so He has made your sins His own and has made His righteousness yours.'[68]

With this brief background, it becomes easier to understand how Luther, motivated by a 'zeal for the truth and the desire to bring it to light',[69] felt that he was obligated to expose how vain it was 'to trust in salvation by indulgence letters . . .'.[70] By the end of 1517, Luther's theological thinking was increasingly becoming centered in 'the most holy gospel of the glory and grace of God'.[71] He had given ample evidence in his lectures on Romans that he had parted company with the theology of human merit. Hence, before ever he stepped upon the public stage of history, there was implicit in his understanding of the doctrine of salvation certain principles which, if carried to their logical conclusions, could serve to undermine the foundation of those claims which gave the Roman church its peculiar authority.

Generally speaking, the medieval ecclesiastical system had made the church an institution which was indispensable in the divine scheme of redemption. A doctrine of salvation by merit and an institutional doctrine of the church were theologically inseparable. By mid-1518, Luther had come to believe that salvation was by grace through faith apart from meritorious works. By faith those who believed were made 'one spirit and one body with Christ'.[72] Faith, and faith alone, became the key to participation in the benefits of Christ's righteousness. The sacraments were seen as 'signs of grace', and were efficacious only when accompanied by faith.[73]

There can be little doubt that Luther, by the end of 1518, was on the road to a concept of the church which was taking him farther away from that held by his opponents.[74] It is difficult to say to what extent he was consciously engaged in developing a new formulation of the doctrine of the church,

but he made it clear before the end of 1518 that he har-
boured no sympathy with the idea that the institution
headed by the pope at Rome was the one and only true
church. He referred to it as the 'church', or more specifically
as the 'Roman church', but he viewed it as one church
among other churches.[75] It had become a 'widow of Christ',
that is, separated from Christ, and in need of reformation.[76]

The question of the position of the pope was more
thoroughly dealt with in 1519 and 1520. By this time Luther
rejected both the doctrine of the primacy and any claim of
infallibility associated with the Roman see.[77] In the *Resolu-
tiones Lutherianae super proposititionibus suis Lipsiae dis-
putatis*, he left no questions about his attitude towards the
authority of the pope. Papal power did not exist by divine
right.[78] It was the result of history and custom. Whatever
power the Roman church might possess by divine right, the
same power was equally possessed by all other churches.[79]
He contended that there was no divine basis for the distinction between priests, bishops, archbishops, patriarchs or
popes.[80] This also rested on history, custom and law. The
whole structure of the medieval ecclesiastical system was
now without foundation. If the papacy did not exist by
divine right, then it could not be above historical judgement.

From 1521 to 1541, a period of twenty years, Luther's
gradual elaboration of the nature of the church did not
depart from its essentially spiritual nature. The true church
was a spiritual reality, visible only to men of faith. If the
word 'church' was used to describe an external structure
or an ecclesiastical order which all men were able to perceive,
it took on a different meaning. These two ideas were kept
separate. Belonging to an external ecclesiastical group was
no guarantee of membership of the true spiritual church.
There was little variation in these sentiments even in the
last years of his life.

In his last great treatise *Against the Roman Papacy, an
Institution of the Devil* (1545) Luther dealt particularly
with papal claims. It was divided into three parts: (1) The
question of papal supremacy; (2) the right to judge and

depose the popes; and (3) the claim that the pope brought
the reign of the Roman Empire from the Greeks to the
Germans.[81] This polemical treatise, perhaps the most bitter
of Luther's writings, made it plain that he believed the
papacy to be an institution founded by the devil.[82] It was
not established by the temporal authority because that
'does not have the power to do this in the kingdom of
God'.[83] It was not the work of the spiritual powers, for
the bishops and councils had fought against it.[84] Because
it did not come from the church, and it did not come from
the temporal authority, Luther concluded that it came
from the devil.[85] By a detailed analysis of many Scripture
passages, especially of Matthew 16 and John 21:15, and
by a consideration of historical events and papal decrees,
Luther built his case against the papacy. In the conclusion
to Part I, he wrote, 'We know that in Christendom it has
been so arranged that all churches are equal, and there is
only one single church of Christ in the world, as we pray,
"I believe in one holy, Christian church." The reason is
this: wherever there is a church, anywhere in the whole
world, it still has no other gospel and Scripture, no other
baptism and communion, no other faith and Spirit, no
other Christ and God, no other Lord's prayer and prayer,
no other hope and eternal life than we have here in our
church in Wittenberg. And their bishops are equal to our
bishops, pastors or preachers; none is lord or servant of the
other; they all have the same kind and heart; and everything belonging to the church is equal.'[86]

Overall, what Luther said in this treatise was principally
an elaboration of what he had written in 1520–1521. The
main difference was in the increased animosity towards the
papacy. Luther called the papacy 'my great anguish' (*meine
grosse Anfechtung*). He was convinced that it could not be
considered a neutral institution. If anything, it was antichristian and demonic. It was entangled in secular and
political matters. It brought souls into fear and bondage
with its legalism. It exalted the traditions of men above
the Word of God.

In spite of everything Luther said about the papacy, he was willing to admit that there were true Christians in the Roman church. This was simply because the Christian church and the Roman church were not one and the same thing.[87] The treatise served to bring out the difference between them. According to Luther, the church remained primarily a spiritual entity. His emphasis was placed against the extravagant claims made by the supporters of the papal view of the church. Their claims made the church to be synonymous with the ecclesiastical institution headed by the pope.[88] Luther continued in his belief that the church was 'the communion of saints'. It was a 'spiritual, living assembly' of people who had believed the gospel and who owned Christ as their Sovereign.[89] The doctrine of the church which he put forward in this treatise was essentially the same as that which appeared in his other Reformation writings. He closed the treatise with reference to his desire to write more on the subject of 'devilish popery', but he died before ever this was accomplished.[90]

Luther's departure from papal thinking about the church remained firmly fixed throughout his whole Reformation career. To state it simply, he could not identify the papal church with the true church of Christ, because it did not give heed to the Word of the Lord and did not teach true doctrine. 'Heretofore,' he declared, 'the papacy alone wanted to be called the church . . . but they are nothing else than the very opponents and enemies of Christ, the persecutors and destroyers of His kingdom.'[91] The pope claimed to be the vicar of Christ for the people of God because he supposedly sat in the seat of the apostles Peter and Paul.[92] 'Even a dog or a swine', exclaimed Luther, 'can sit in the place of St Peter.'[93] The point here was not one of acerbity. Luther wanted it to be understood that just as an ecclesiastical organization in itself did not constitute a true church, so historical continuity by itself could not be the sole distinction between the true and false church. Any taunt such as 'Where was your church before Luther?' obviously fails to appreciate Luther's view of what constituted the true church.

Luther clearly perceived that there was a difference
between the *ecclesia* of the New Testament and the institutionalized Roman church. A great part of the reformation
controversy raged because of Luther's reaction against the
quid pro quo which tried to identify them.[94] Theologians
like Eck and Prierias were adamant in teaching that the
church which Christ established was conterminous with
the institution headed by the pope. All the rights and
privileges ascribed to the church of the New Testament
were assigned to the papal institution. With this view Luther
had no quarter. Yet it is clear that he saw historical continuity from the first-century Christian church until his day.
In fact, he believed that the church dated back to Adam
and Eve,[95] and that it would always exist on earth 'until
the Last Day'.[96] Even throughout the darkness of the papal
period God had preserved a remnant of His people.[97]

Luther believed that the historical church had become
alienated from the church of the New Testament. He objected to Roman Catholic Christianity in the light of his
biblically oriented theology. It is important that this be
understood, for the principle which motivated Luther in his
view of the church was 'the determination to go back to and
renew the original life of Christianity'.[98] Luther realized
that the institutional church of his day had developed by a
long process of transformation out of the original Christian
society of the New Testament. The papacy itself was a
prime example of the entrance of human traditions into
the life of the church. Luther recognized this fact even in
the formative years of the Reformation. In his *Defence and
Explanation of All the Articles,* written in response to the
bull *Exsurge Domine,* he boldly asserted that 'The papacy
is a human invention of which God knows nothing.'[99]
Certainly, there was nothing of it in Holy Scripture. As to
its historical inception, it dated back to about the time of
Jerome.[100] These human traditions, which Luther spoke of
as 'outward pretensions and man-made laws', had been
responsible for the origin and development of all manner
of 'abominations and errors' in the church.[101] But in spite

of the doctrinal perversions of which the Roman church was guilty, Luther held that the true church had perpetuated itself and was still present in his day, although it took a sort of faith-vision to recognize it.

Any attempt to undo the ecclesiastical traditions which had developed throughout history did not, in Luther's mind, contradict the historical continuity of the true church.[102] The church existed in his day and it sustained a direct historical link with the New Testament apostles.[103] Believing this, he taught that there was no salvation outside of the church, for in his own words: 'Christ is to be found only where the Word is preached, and the Word is not preached except in the Christian church.'[104] A sinner came to Christ only by means of the gospel which was proclaimed in the church. Luther was not teaching that membership of the church organization was the condition of salvation. To make him say this would be to read him out of context. In his own words, he said, 'Anyone who is to find Christ must first find the church . . . Now the church is not wood and stone, but the company of people who believe in Christ . . . Christ is certainly in their midst. Outside the Christian church there is no truth, no Christ and no salvation.'[105]

As far as the unity of the church was concerned, it was not a matter dependent upon maintaining the *status quo* of the ecclesiastical system. This would make it contingent upon that which was of human invention. Instead Luther saw the unity of the church in connection with the gospel of Christ.[106] He did not despise organizational and liturgical order, but such things did not make the church. As long as the gospel was proclaimed through the spoken word and the sacraments, the church continued. The gospel might not be proclaimed altogether purely, but where it evoked faith, there existed the church.

The church, then, for Luther was essentially a spiritual fellowship of believing souls who had been born again by the Holy Spirit through faith in the gospel.[108] In this definition of the church, the most commonly repeated terms were those which involved personal relationships rather than an impersonal organization. He saw the church as a 'people', 'God's people', 'the community of believers', and the '*communio sanctorum*'. It existed on the earth by the Word of God and by faith. Its uninterrupted continuity was not in the succession of bishops, but in the succession of the faithful. He believed that this interpretation of the church was a recovery of the early Christian idea as revealed in the Holy Scriptures.

Luther's appeal to the authority of Holy Scripture is the master key to understanding his conflict with the hierarchy of the Roman church. From this divinely inspired source he derived his concept of the church. As this became clear to his mind, he realized that he could not compromise with that view of the church which was bound to the exclusive prerogatives of papal claims. Also, since these same claims supported the 'hog-theologians', with their sacramental-merit theology, revolt was inevitable.

Here, in the final analysis, lay the basic cause of the Reformation. Essentially, it centered in theological controversy between two opposing systems of salvation, which could not be reconciled, since two incompatible criteria were vying with each other as sources of authority. The one was related inextricably to papal claims and the other was determined solely by appeal to Holy Scripture. It should be self-evident to any thinking person that there can be no hope of repairing the breach between Roman Catholicism and so-called traditional Protestantism while each continues to hold to its own distinctive court of authority. There is perhaps no theological question more important in this or in any age than that which lies behind the issue of authority. In this connection, Edward J. Carnell asked, 'Do we find the truth by submitting to the church, or do we find the church by submitting to the truth?'[109] The Roman church defends the first possibility while those in the Reformation tradition defend the second. Luther's own position was made very clear at the Diet of Worms in 1521. Carlyle called it the greatest moment in modern history. Before the emperor himself, and the great ecclesiastical representatives of papal power, Luther was confronted by a variety of his books. He was asked to repudiate them, and to recant of the errors which they supposedly contained. He answered, 'Unless I am convicted by Scripture and plain reason (since I believe neither in the authority of popes and councils, for they have often erred and contradicted themselves) I am conquered by the Scriptures quoted by me, and my conscience is captive to the Word of God, I cannot and I will not recant anything, for to go against conscience is unsafe and dangerous. Here I stand, I can do no otherwise. God help me. Amen.'[110]

NOTES

[1] Trevor Gervase Jalland, *The Church and the Papacy* (London: Society for Promoting Christian Knowledge, 1944), p. 436.

[2] Jaroslav Pelikan and Helmut T. Lehmann, eds. *Luther's Works,* 55 vols (Concordia Publishing House and Muhlenburg Press, 1955—) XXXI, 263. Further reference abbreviated to *L.W.*

[3] *L.W.,* XLVIII, 89.

[4] *Ibid.,* 100.

[5] *Ibid.,* 101.

[6] *L.W.,* XXVII, 153.

[7] *L.W.,* XXXI, 25.

[8] *L.W.,* XLVIII, 68.

[9] *L.W.,* XXVII, 153.

[10] Christopher Henry Dawson, *The Dividing of Christendom* (New York: Sheed and Ward, 1965), pp. 79, 80.

[11] Philip Hughes, *A History of the Church* (3 vols; New York: Sheed and Ward, 1947), III, 488.

[12] *L.W.,* XXXI, 28, 31.

[13] Hans J. Hillerbrand, *The Reformation* (New York: Harper and Row, 1964), pp. 41—43.

[14] *Ibid.,* 43.

[15] *L.W.,* XLVIII, 46.

[16] *Ibid.,* 47.

[17] *Ibid.*

[18] *Ibid.*

[19] Albert Hyma, *New Light on Martin Luther* (Grand Rapids: Wm B. Eerdmans Publishing Company, 1958), p. 80.

[20] Hubert Jedin, *A History of the Council of Trent,* trans. Ernest Graf (St Louis: B. Herder Book Company, 1957), I, 114, 158, 171.

[21] *L.W.,* XLI, 234.

[22] The word means 'dagger points' and it comes from Origen's use of such signs to denote questionable statements in contemporary literature.

²³ E. G. Schwiebert, *Luther and His Times* (St Louis: Concordia Publishing House, 1950), p. 322.

²⁴ *L.W.*, XLI, 234.

²⁵ E. G. Schwiebert, *op. cit.*, p. 334.

²⁶ Lucien Febvre, *Martin Luther: A Destiny* (New York: E. P. Dutton and Company, Inc., 1929), p. 140.

²⁷ *L.W.*, XXXI, 215.

²⁸ *Ibid.*, 225.

²⁹ Roland H. Bainton, *The Reformation of the Sixteenth Century* (Boston: The Beacon Press, 1952), p. 41.

³⁰ *Ibid.*, 30, 261.

³¹ *Ibid.*, 261.

³² *L.W.*, XXXI, 262.

³³ *Ibid.*

³⁴ *Ibid.*, 278.

³⁵ *Ibid.*, 281.

³⁶ *Ibid.* Luther appears to have erroneously inferred that Gregory I was the first to have received the title of 'Pope' as head of the entire church and that previous bishops had not used the title.

³⁷ *Ibid.*, 239, 282.

³⁸ Henry Denzinger, *Enchiridion Symbolorum, The Sources of Catholic Dogma*, trans. Roy J. Deferrari (St Louis: B. Herder Book Company, 1957), p. 239.

³⁹ *Ibid.*

⁴⁰ *Ibid.*

⁴¹ *L.W.*, XLVIII, 105.

⁴² *L.W.*, XXXI, 152.

⁴³ *L.W.*, XLVIII, 114. The development of Luther's doctrine of the Antichrist is considered in John M. Headley, *Luther's View of Church History* (New Haven: Yale University Press, 1963), pp. 181–223.

⁴⁴ *L.W.*, XXXI, 318.

⁴⁵ *Ibid.*, 321–322.

⁴⁶ *L.W.*, XXVII, 153, 158.

⁴⁷ *Ibid.*, 156.

⁴⁸ Works of Martin Luther, 6 vols (Philadelphia: A. J. Holman Company, 1915–32), II, 10. Further reference abbreviated to *W.M.L.*

⁴⁹ *Ibid.*, 37.

⁵⁰ Preserved Smith, *The Life and Letters of Martin Luther* (New York: Houghton Mifflin Company, 1911), p. 73.

⁵¹ *W.M.L.*, *op. cit.*, II, 58.

⁵² Henry Eyster Jacobs, *Martin Luther, The Hero of the Reformation, 1483–1546* (New York: G. P. Putnam's Sons, 1898), pp. 413, 414.

⁵³ *L.W.*, XLVIII, 183.

⁵⁴ Hubert Jedin, *op. cit.*, p. 177.

⁵⁵ *L.W.*, XLVIII, 192.

⁵⁶ *L.W.*, XXXI, 348.

⁵⁷ *L.W.*, XXXII, 82.

⁵⁸ Etienne Gilson, *Reason and Revelation in the Middle Ages* (New York: Charles Scribner's Sons, 1938), p. 87.

⁵⁹ Ockhamism and 'nominalism' are often used interchangeably, but according to Heiko A. Oberman, a noted authority in this field, 'It is more correct to

distinguish between them', the former being a more highly developed form of the latter — Heiko A. Oberman, 'Some Notes on the Theology of Nominalism with Attention to its Relation to the Renaissance,' *The Harvard Theological Review*, LIII (January 1960), 48.

[60] Heiko A. Oberman, *Harvest of Medieval Theology* (Cambridge, Mass.: Harvard University Press, 1963), p. 180.

[61] Albert Hyma, *Luther's Theological Development from Erfurt to Augsburg* (New York: F. S. Crofts and Co., 1928), p. 40.

[62] Philip Watson has an excellent summary of these points in his work, *Let God be God* (Philadelphia: Fortress Press, 1947), pp. 15, 16.

[63] Hans J. Hillerbrand, *The Reformation* (New York: Harper & Row, 1964), p. 24.

[64] Preserved Smith, *The Life and Letters of Martin Luther* (New York: Houghton Mifflin Company, 1911), p. 15.

[65] Heiko A. Oberman, '*Iustitia Christi*, and *Iustitia Dei*, Luther and the Scholastic Doctrines of Justification,' *Harvard Theological Review*, LIX (January 1966), 7.

[66] Gordon Rupp, *The Righteousness of God* (New York: Philosophical Library, Inc., 1953), p. 123.

[67] Preserved Smith, *op. cit.*, p. 24.

[68] *L.W.*, XLVIII, 12, 13.

[69] *L.W.*, XXXI, 25.

[70] *Ibid.*, 30.

[71] *Ibid.*, 31.

[72] *Ibid.*, 190.

[73] *Ibid.*, 193.

[74] This is evident both in the *Explanations of the Ninety-Five Theses*, and in the *Proceedings at Augsburg*.

[75] *L.W.*, XXXI, 152.

[76] *Ibid.*, 237, 250.

[77] *Ibid.*, 152, 171.

[78] *W.A.*, II, 201.

[79] *Ibid.*, 208.

[80] *Ibid.*, 432.

[81] *Ibid.*, 289, 290.

[82] *Ibid.*, 296.

[83] *Ibid.*, 298.

[84] *Ibid.*, 299.

[85] *Ibid.*, 301.

[86] *Ibid.*, 358.

[87] *Ibid.*, 296, 311.

[88] *Ibid.*, 293, 294.

[89] *Ibid.*, 308, 309.

[90] *Ibid.*, 376.

[91] *L.W.*, XIII, 286.

[92] *L.W.*, IV, 348.

[93] *Ibid.*

[94] Jaroslav Pelikan, *Obedient Rebels* (New York: Harper and Row, 1964), p. 27.

[95] *L.W.*, XIII, 90.

[96] *Ibid.*, 324.

[97] *W.M.L.*, V, 269.

[98] Emil Brunner, *The Misunderstanding of the Church*, trans. Harold Knight (London: Lutterworth Press, 1952), p. 96.

[99] *L.W.*, XXXII, 82.

[100] *L.W.*, LI, 78.

[101] *L.W.*, XXXII, 7.

[102] Emil Brunner, *op. cit.*, p. 97.

[103] Geddes MacGregor, *Corpus Christi, The Nature of the Church According to the Reformed Tradition* Philadelphia: The Westminster Press, 1958), p. 8.

[104] *W.M.L.*, II, 373.

[105] Lennart Pinomaa, *Faith Victorious*, trans. Walter J. Kukkonen (Philadelphia: Fortress Press, 1963), p. 117.

[106] John M. Headley, *Luther's View of Church History* (New Haven and London: Yale University Press, 1963), p. 29.

[107] Ernst Troeltsch, *op. cit.*, p. 478.

[108] *L.W.*, IV, 348—349.

[109] Edward John Carnell, *The Case for Biblical Christianity*, ed. Ronald H. Nash (Grand Rapids: William B. Eerdmans, 1969), p. 26.

[110] John C. L . Gieseler, *A Text-Book of Church History*, trans., Henry B. Smith, 5 vols. (New York: Harper & Brothers, 1876) IV, 57. The Latin and the German from which the quotation was translated is as follows:

Nisi convictus fuero testimoniis Scripturarum, aut ratione evidente (nam neque Papae, neque Conciliis solis credo, cum constet eos errasse saepius, et sibi ipsis contradixisse); victus sum Scripturis a me adductis, captaque est conscientia in verbis Dei, revocare neque possum, neque volo quidquam, cum contra conscientiam agere neque tutum sit neque integrum. Hie stehe ich, ich kann nicht anders, Gott helf mir, Amen.

4
The development after the Reformation

The final page of Geoffrey Barraclough's book *The Medieval Papacy* contains the judgement that 'The medieval papacy ended in bankruptcy.' Furthermore, he pondered the possibility 'whether but for Luther, it might not have carried medieval Christendom — or western Christendom — into bankruptcy with it'.[1] Luther was by no means the first to call for a reformation of the church. Throughout the whole of the fifteenth century, and on into the sixteenth century, there was much discussion among thoughtful men concerning the need to reform the abuses within the Roman church, and particularly within the Curia itself. Francesco Guicciardini (1483—1540) wrote that, 'So much evil cannot be said of the Roman Curia that more does not deserve to be said of it, for it is an infamy, an example of the shame and wickedness of the world.'[2] Moreover, rather than put themselves at the head of such a movement, the popes appeared inclined, more often than not, to be actively involved in seeking to prevent it. Not only the popes, but the cardinals also, according to Guicciardini, were suspicious of the reforms a council might introduce.[3] Following the Reformation, the emperor himself added his weight to insist on a council, but his assurances to protect papal interests fell on deaf ears. In the opinion of Hubert Jedin, who wrote the definitive history of the Council of Trent (1545—1563), this general antipathy towards a reforming council was a dreadful mistake.[4]

Ever since the days of Pius II and *Execrabilis,* papal opposition to the theory of reforming councils had become almost endemic. If anything, the Reformation had served to intensify the antagonism between curialist and conciliarist forces. Yet, at the same time the hierarchy of the Roman church was on the horns of a dilemma for, with Luther's victories and the widespread acceptance of his teachings, retrenchment was hardly an advisable course of action. More fitting would be a counter-offensive, if not a 'Counter-Reformation'. It was obviously a time for extraordinary measures if the spread of Protestantism was to be halted. How best then to offset the exigencies of what to Roman Catholic eyes was a serious threat to the very foundation of the church?

The first serious attempt at some degree of reform was made by Leo X's non-Italian successor, Adrian VI (1522–1523). However, it was doomed to failure. First of all, Adrian VI's pontificate was too short. Second, he found the corruption at Rome to be invincible. Third, his prescribed medication to help cure the illness was viewed as being worse than the disease itself. Rather than mourning, there was much relief at his passing. His successor, Clement VII (1523–1534), a descendent of the Florentine Medici, was a vacillating pusillanimous type of individual who did little more than toy with the idea of a reforming council. When a rumour of such a council caused the prices of saleable ecclesiastical offices to dwindle, he quickly squashed the rumour. One of his contemporaries described his pontificate as being 'one of scruples, considerations and discords, of buts and ifs and thens and moreovers, and plenty of words without effect'.[5] Of course, Clement VII was not alone in his aversion to a council. Aleander, a papal legate, advised him, 'Never offer a council, never refuse it directly. On the contrary, show you are willing to comply with the request, but stress the difficulties in the way. Thus you will be able to ward it off.'[6] The primary reason for papal opposition to reforming councils remained essentially the same. It was basically a fear of infringement of pontifical power. Why run the risk of reviving conciliarism?

Pressure for a reforming council continued to mount. Nationalism was on the rise. During Clement VII's reign,

England repudiated papal authority and royal supremacy became an accomplished fact. The only countries remaining solidly in the papal camp were Italy and Spain. However, with the pontificate of Paul III (1534—1549), there was a noticeable turning-point. No sooner was he elected than he announced that the work of reform would begin. He appointed a commission of nine cardinals to recommend guidelines for the reform of the church. In their report (1537) they pulled no punches. They were respectful, but they made it clear that in their opinion the great ills of the church were traceable to former pontiffs who had all too readily abused the power of their office. Contarini, one of the commission, candidly urged a complete renovation of the Curia. He even went so far as to declare that the 'Lutherans were entirely justified' in comparing the holy see with the Babylonish captivity. The evil practices which had alienated so many men came from papal pretensions of absolute power. The rule of St Peter and his successors was to be exercised, not according to any pope's own pleasure, 'but in obedience to the rule of reason, of God's command, and to the law of love, referring everything to God, and doing all in consideration of the common good only'.[7]

Pope Paul III was apparently sympathetic towards the reform of the entire church organization by means of a general council. His efforts were not without some opposition or caution from certain prelates who feared curtailment of both power and income. One such warned him, 'Commit yourself to nothing until it is agreed that the pope is absolute master of the council.'[8] Under the prodding of the emperor, Paul III did call a council which eventually met at Trent, a little town in the north of Italy, but still within the confines of the Holy Roman Empire. The Germans were opposed to an Italian city because they distrusted papal influence. Even the Protestants were invited but refused to attend. One of Luther's reasons for his work *Against the Roman Papacy, an Institution of the Devil* (1545) was to justify the refusal of the Protestants to accept the invitation. The council met in three separate sessions, 1545—1547, 1551—1552 and

1562—1563.   During the second period the Protestants
did send a delegation which presented a confession of faith,
but they refused to recognize the authority of the council.
It was the longest council in the history of the Roman
church, as well as the last for over three hundred years.
According to McBrien, 'Until Vatican II, twentieth-century
Catholicism was shaped more by the Council of Trent than
by any other historically tangible event or force.'[9]

In general review, it is quite apparent that there was
throughout the whole course of the council a more or less
hidden struggle between the defenders of papal power and
the conciliarists. Father Paul Sarpi, the Roman Catholic
historian of Trent, judged that the council was a failure, if
not a fraud. Apart from the packing of the membership
with pro-papal Italian yes-men, Philip Schaff described the
members of the council as being 'not distinguished for learning or piety, but were a set of wrangling monks and canonists and minions of the pope'.[10] Another measure which
aimed at ensuring papal control of the council was that of
granting the initiative to the papal legates. While the council
was not under the immediate control of the pope, there was
frequent communication from Rome, to the extent that the
French ambassador jested of the Holy Ghost coming to Trent
in the mailbags from Rome.[11] Pius IV (1559—1565) during
the final sessions was able to keep a majority of Italians on
the council, and in the final clash on papal supremacy he con-
trolled the decisions by only seventy-one votes to sixty-six.

There were three basic tasks confronting those attending
the Council of Trent: (1) The settlement of religious disputes
by doctrinal decisions; (2) the reform of ecclesiastical abuses;
and (3) the discussion of a crusade against the infidel. Need-
less to say, the first two tasks were the cause of stormy
debate. At times the controversy actually raged into physical
violence. At one point dissension became so heated that one
bishop tore the beard of another. In the third period of the
council, contention over rules for the improvement of the
convents waxed so hot that the representatives of the various
factions fought in the streets of Trent. During this third and

final period it was obvious that the council was under the control of the papacy. This was made evident by the request of the council that all decrees should be confirmed by the pope. This was done by Pius IV (1559–1565) one month after the council ended on 26 January 1564 in the bull *Benedictus Deus.* Before the year was over, he issued another important bull *Injunctum nobis,* which became the *Tridentine Profession of Faith.* Among the opening words of this profession of faith, which was to be recited publicly by all bishops and beneficed clergy of the 'Holy Roman Church', there is a startling statement with regard to the church's authority to interpret the Holy Scriptures: 'I acknowledge the sacred Scripture according to that sense which Holy Mother Church has held and holds, to whom it belongs to decide upon the true sense and interpretation of the Holy Scriptures, nor will I ever receive and interpret the Scripture except according to the unanimous consent of the fathers.'[12]

Among the other ecclesiastical traditions included in this profession of faith, which, according to the documents of Vatican Council II (1962–1963), were still binding upon Roman Catholics in the twentieth century, there were listed: the seven sacraments, transubstantiation, purgatory, veneration and invocation of saints, veneration also of relics, of images of Christ, of the ever-virgin mother of God, and of saints and, lastly, the power of indulgences. Those who embraced and received all the definitions and declarations of the 'holy Council of Trent' were professing the 'true Catholic faith' without which no one could be in a state of salvation. Required of those making this public profession was also the following credal oath: 'I recognize the holy catholic and apostolic Roman church as the mother and mistress of all churches; and I vow and swear true obedience to the Roman pontiff, and successor of blessed Peter, the chief of the apostles and the representative [*vicarius*] of Jesus Christ.'[13]

Not only did the Council of Trent and the *Tridentine Profession of Faith* close the door to reconciliation with

the Protestants, they also created what Trevor Jalland called
'a siege mentality'. As in times of severe national crisis,
constitutions are suspended and dictators with absolute
authority are accepted, so among those remaining within
the Roman camp the acceptance of papal absolutism
became a condition of survival.[14] The analogy seems to be
very appropriate, for there was a hasty reconstruction of
doctrinal fortifications to counteract the threat from
Protestantism. There was the imposition of a more centralized discipline. New religious orders came into existence,
such as the Society of Jesus founded by Ignatius Loyola in
1540. In the constitution of this new order, the image of
militant warfare was projected and a special oath of
allegiance to the Roman pontiff was a prerequisite. About
this same time, 1542 to be exact, the infamous Roman
Inquisition was established. Related to the Inquisition, the
Roman *Index of Prohibited Books* was promulgated. All in
all, what was happening was that the old papal claims were
being reasserted and shored up by a new coalition of forces
and by a reformed papacy.

Rated high in this coalition of forces, which moulded
Roman Catholic thinking at the end of the sixteenth, and
beginning of the seventeenth centuries, must be the writings
of Robert Bellarmine (1542–1621). During the high tide of
the Counter-Reformation he was the principal theologian
of the Society of Jesus. Next to the Council of Trent, his
work has probably had more influence on the development
of Roman Catholic theology in modern history than any
other single factor. He was uncompromisingly ultramontane
in his papal views. He viewed the church in a monarchical
manner, with the pope as supreme head and the Roman
prelates as the aristocracy. The Roman pontiff was universal
teacher of the church and in this role was incapable of error.
All councils were subordinate to him. He was to rule the
church with the plenitude of ecclesiastical jurisdiction, and
could not be liable to judgement by others. As supreme
ruler, he had the right to impose laws on all the faithful and
to compel obedience even by means of the death penalty.

Anyone familiar with the subsequent development of papal views of power, particularly towards the end of the nineteenth century, can hardly fail to notice how Bellarmine was in advance of his time.

Notwithstanding the 'siege mentality' of the Counter-Reformation, the historical ebb and flow of events and forces throughout the seventeenth and eighteenth centuries contributed to a steady decline in papal power. Even the popes of the period, at least according to one sympathetic brief study of the papacy, 'although themselves worthy men, were not for the most part men of great intellectual stature or strong character'.[15] These were the years when the Roman church was troubled by such movements as Jansenism, Gallicanism, Josephism and political Liberalism.

The Jansenists took their name from Cornelius Otto Jansen (1585–1638). The movement itself is not easy to explain. In some ways it resembled the Puritan and even the Quaker movements which were Protestant contemporaries. It might even be described as a sort of Roman Catholic revivalist phenomenon which gave expression to the need for a religion of the 'inner soul'. There was a stress upon conversion and the necessity and irresistibility of grace, that is, a sort of 'Calvinizing of Catholicism'. Had it not been for its open attack on the moral laxity of the Jesuits, and its tendency to play down the supremacy of the pope, it might have elicited no great alarm. Jansen's book *Augustinus,* which was published posthumously in 1640, was condemned by Pope Urban VIII (1623–1644) in 1642. Five propositions which supposedly summed up the Jansenist position were condemned by Pope Innocent X (1644–1655) in the bull *Cum occasione* (1653). One noteworthy result of the quarrel was the work of Blaise Pascal, the *Provincial Letters,* which added ammunition to the Jansenists in their battle against the Jesuits.

In certain ways Gallicanism looked like the old caesaro-papism only in modern dress. The Byzantine emperors had seen their temporal power within a broad spiritual framework where they were charged with the supervisory

protection of the Christian faith. The new caesaropapism
went a step further and tended to claim complete control
over the church. Even papal power was to be made subject
to the absolutism of the royal will. King Louis XIV (1643–
1715) asserted this *droit de regale* in his conflict with Pope
Innocent XI (1676–1689) over the drawing of revenues
from vacant bishoprics and his claim to the right of nomination to these sees. Of course, Innocent XI contested the
claim and declared invalid the acts of bishops thus appointed.
The French clergy supported the king and in 1692 stood
behind the *Gallican Declaration* which proclaimed that
kings could not be subject to ecclesiastical power in temporal matters and that they could not be deposed 'directly
or indirectly' by the authority of the church. In this connection, it was also declared that subjects could not be
dispensed from obedience nor absolved from the oath of
allegiance to their kings by ecclesiastical decrees. Particularly noteworthy in this *Declaration* is Article II, which,
while it conceded that 'the plenitude of power in spiritual
matters possessed by St Peter and his successors' did remain,
it did so in accordance with the decrees laid down by the
Council of Constance.[16] Also, in Article IV, obvious restrictions were placed on the pope's magisterial office: 'Although
the pope has the chief voice in questions of faith, and his
decrees apply to all churches and to each particular church,
yet his decision is not unalterable unless the consent of the
church is given.'[17]

Similar sentiments, such as these contained in the *Gallican
Articles,* were now becoming common. They were being
expressed and bandied about by kings and scholars. One
work, written under the pseudonym of Febronius, which
achieved widespread popularity and went quickly through
a number of editions, advocated a constitutional theory of
papal authority and urged the abandonment of all papal
claims based on the *False Decretals.* Within a few years of
its appearance (1763) the 'omnipotent' state appeared to
have the papacy under tight control. In the case of Austria,
under the Emperor Joseph II (1765–1790), the church

became little more than a department of the state and virtually every aspect of ecclesiastical life was subjected to
government regulation. Joseph II even contemplated a
complete renunciation of papal power.

In revolutionary France, the church fared no better. The
National Constituent Assembly voted for the Civil Constitution of the clergy which provided for the election of bishops
and pastors by popular vote, denying any papal influence in
their choice. Under the Directory and Napoleon, popes were
imprisoned and cardinals were arrested and scattered. Uni-
laterally, Napoleon published the *Organic Articles* which
declared that all papal acts and bulls, also decrees of general
councils, should be submitted to the government for
approval.

Political Liberalism, which favoured constitutional parliamentary type government, also breathed out threatenings
against any symptom of papal absolutism. But papal reaction
was soon forthcoming. Claims of papal supremacy were by
no means dead. The task was not an easy one. How best
could the Roman church secure its necessary freedom in the
world to permit the continuance of its mission? This could
scarcely be done without dealing with the basic question of
the pope's position and the extent of his power.

It was not until the nineteenth century, during the pontificate of Pius IX (1846—1878), that the question of the extent
of papal power was officially settled. There can be little
doubt, however, that it was Pius IX himself who manoeuvred
the whole thing.[18] In his first year as pope, on 9 November,
he issued an encyclical which declared his infallibility in
matters dealing with faith and morals. Also worthy of mention is the fact that in this same letter he called Mary
'*immaculata*'. The dogma of the immaculate conception of
Mary was proclaimed eight years later on 8 December 1854.
Papal authority on the basis of tradition alone was the main
force in the proclamation of this dogma. That such was the
case is fully acknowledged by the Jesuit Schrader: 'It is an
act to which no former pontificate can show a parallel; for
the pope defined the dogma of his own sovereign authority,

without the co-operation of a council; and this independent action involves practically, if not formally, another dogmatic definition, namely that the pope is infallible in matters of faith in his own person and not merely when presiding at a council.'[19]

The next important step of Pius IX in preparation for the formal definition of the dogma of papal infallibility was the issuance of the *Syllabus of Errors.* This consisted of an authoritative condemnation of some eighty supposed errors that were prevalent in the modern world. On 6 December 1864, together with a special encyclical *Quanta Cura*, this *Syllabus* was sent to all the prelates of the Roman church. The encyclical concluded with an expression of confidence in the power of the immaculate virgin, who is described as standing on the right hand of her Son, attired in a dress of gold with a cloak of divers colours, and as being the destroyer of all heresies in the universe. The religious phraseology of both documents reflects an obvious logical interdependence. Their contents are indispensable in tracing the development of papal views of power, for they reveal quite clearly that there was in fact little or no change from that of the medieval viewpoint. Ecclesiastical authority rests essentially in the pope, who is not only head of the church, but is also above the state. The duty of governments is to protect the church, and to compel and punish all who do not conform to its decrees. Papal power must not be limited to faith and morals. Even in the early years of the twentieth century the *Syllabus* was very much alive. In 1903, Cardinal Archbishop Fischer of Koln wrote in a pastoral letter to his clergy, 'The *Syllabus of Errors* is a touchstone of our own time; by which we can decide what agrees with Catholic truth and what contradicts it.'[20]

Two days before the issue of the *Syllabus*, Pope Pius IX made known to the Congregation of Rites the idea of holding a general council. There was a great deal of secrecy associated with the formative planning stages of this idea, and apparently it was only those on the inside who knew that the main objective of the council would be the definition of

papal infallibility. It was no mere coincidence that the date
chosen for the opening of the council was 8 December 1869.
This was the same date as the dogma of the immaculate conception and the issue of the *Syllabus*. Protestants were
invited to attend, but in a manner fitting for 'prodigal child-
ren'. Protestantism was not to be discussed, for sentence was
long ago pronounced. It was a *chose jugée*.[21] From the very
beginning to the very end, the First Vatican Council was
geared by papal machinations to railroad through the doctrine of infallibility.[22] There is hardly a better example of a
petitio principii in all history. Where was the rationale in asking the council to define a doctrine which only the pope
himself could define? As one French journalist observed, 'It
was a true master stroke to set the papal infallibility in opera-
tion before it is proclaimed as dogma.'[23]

There was, of course, a great deal of controversy connected with the dogma of papal infallibility. Much of it dealt
with the question of historical precedents. Archbishop
Manning argued that since the doctrine was not mentioned
between the fifth and the fifteenth century it meant that it
must have been universally accepted. In the opposing camp,
Dollinger argued exactly the opposite case, attributing the
doctrine to forgeries and fictions. William Gladstone, in his
book *Rome and the Newest Fashions in Religion*, made the
statement that 'The popes had kept up with comparatively
little intermission, for well nigh a thousand years their claim
to dogmatic infallibility . . .'[24] Later, he felt obligated to
retract this statement admitting that it was made 'without
sufficient reflection' and 'with culpable inadvertence'.[25]
After further research he changed his mind exclaiming that,
'I do not deny to the opinion of papal infallibility an active,
though a chequered and intermittent, life exceeding six
centuries.'[26] This would place the historical origins of the
doctrine somewhere in the thirteenth century. The historical
reliability of Gladstone's judgement is to be commended. It
might be remembered that in chapter 1 it was mentioned
that Brian Tierney's book *Origins of Papal Infallibility,
1159—1350*, which was published one hundred years after

Gladstone's work, provided historical evidence that the
association of infallibility with papal authority first came
into play at the end of the thirteenth century. The gist of
Tierney's research is worth recounting.

Writing strictly from a historian's point of view, Tierney
sees no convincing evidence that the doctrine of papal
infallibility formed any part of the theological or canonical
traditions of the Roman church before the thirteenth century. It was first introduced by Pietro Olivi, a Franciscan
master, towards the end of the thirteenth century. Behind
Olivi's thinking was the simple design to limit the capacity
of future popes to cause any damage to the doctrines of the
church. He did this by insisting on the infallibility and
'irreformability' of doctrinal decisions made by preceding
popes. His arguments came into the limelight in the fourteenth century when certain Franciscans found it necessary
in their struggle over the question of poverty to maintain
that certain papal decrees were infallible and immutable.
Later still, the doctrine proved useful in combating conciliarism. In other words, the doctrine was invented in an atmo-
sphere of dissidence to support one party against another.
In similar vein, the popes themselves came to accept it,
sometimes with reluctance, because it suited their conveni-
ence in the circumstances in which they found themselves.
What Tierney has shown is that there is a wide gap between
the medieval theologians and canonists, and the thinking of
Vatican Council I.

One of the most remarkable facts about the final outcome
of Vatican Council I in 1870 was the way the vote went on
the doctrine of papal infallibility. By all outward appear-
ances, and in marked contrast with the Council of Trent,
the final favourable vote was a veritable landslide. Out of
535 prelates who voted, 533 cast affirmative responses. It
should be mentioned that 106 members were absent. Among
the absentees and those opposing the affirmative vote were
cardinals, archbishops, bishops and some of the Roman
church's leading historians — names such as Rauscher,
Schwarzenberg, Conolly, Carboy, Hefele, Ketteler, Kenrick,

Strossmayer, Cerot, Clifton, Dupanloup and, not the least, the highly esteemed Dr Dollinger. These men, along with others, represented no small storehouse of elaborate erudition. Of the 766 prelates in attendance, 541 were from Europe, and of these, 276 came from the Italian peninsula. Gertrude Himmelfarb makes the facetious comment: 'In ecclesiastical statistics, it appeared that twenty learned Germans counted for less than one untutored Italian.'[27] The day before the momentous vote was cast, Dupanloup, one of the opposition leaders, persuaded those yet remaining in Rome to leave in a body and thus avoid casting a negative vote. He had already attempted to persuade the pope to exercise prudence and moderation and to postpone if possible any confirmation of the council's decision with regard to the position and the power of the papal office. Archbishop Haynald of Hungary, in company with Dupanloup, left Rome on the eve of the final session. In the early morning of the historic day, as Dupanloup was opening his breviary, Haynald leaned towards him and said: 'Monseigneur, nous avons fait une grande faute' ('Monseigneur, we have made a great mistake').[28]

Exactly what Haynald intended might be disputed. Did he express concern over being party to the opposition? Did he imply that they should have stayed and registered their negative vote? Whatever he meant, it made no difference to the outcome. On 18 July 1870, the decree contained in the document *The First Dogmatic Constitution Concerning the Church of Christ* was published and approved. The content of this decree merits close consideration. It begins with a brief introduction, followed by four comparatively short chapters. In each of them, with perhaps the exception of the last, which contains the big bone of contention concerning papal infallibility, the basic elements in the Petrine theory are all clearly proclaimed. The first chapter, entitled 'Of the Institution of the Apostolic Primacy in Blessed Peter', minced no words in its explicit claims. Clearly the statements focus upon Peter 'alone' being the one to whom Christ the Lord spoke the words of Matthew 16:18, 19. The decree concludes with the solemn anathema: 'If anyone, therefore, shall say that blessed Peter the apostle was not appointed the prince of all the apostles and the visible head of the whole church militant; or that the same directly and immediately received from the same our Lord Jesus Christ a primacy of honour only, and not of true and proper jurisdiction — let him be anathema.'[29]

The second chapter, headed with the words, 'On the Perpetuity of the Primacy of Blessed Peter in the Roman Pontiff,' is no less explicit. Here is spelled out in unmistakable terms the doctrine of apostolic succession: 'That which the Prince of shepherds and great Shepherd of the sheep, Jesus Christ our Lord, established in the person of the blessed apostle Peter to secure the perpetual welfare and lasting good of the church, must, by the same institution, necessarily remain unceasingly in the church; which, being founded upon the rock, will stand firm to the end of the world. For none can doubt, and it is known to all ages, that the holy and blessed Peter, the prince and chief of the apostles, the pillar of the faith and foundation of the Catholic church, received the keys of the kingdom from our Lord Jesus Christ, the Saviour and Redeemer of mankind, and lives, presides and judges, to this day and always, in his successors the Bishops of the holy see of Rome, which was founded by him, and consecrated by his book . . .

'If, then, any should deny that it is by the institution of Christ the Lord, or by divine right, that blessed Peter should have a perpetual line of successors in the primacy over the universal church, or that the Roman pontiff is the successor of blessed Peter in this primacy — let him be anathema'.[30]

The third chapter, arguing in an apparently logical manner on the premises contained in the preceding two chapters, proceeds to define 'The Power and Nature of the Primacy of the Roman Pontiff'. 'All the faithful of Christ must believe that the holy apostolic see and the Roman pontiff possesses the primacy over the whole world, and that the Roman pontiff is the successor of blessed Peter, prince of the apostles, and is true vicar of Christ, and head of the whole church, and father and teacher of all Christians; and that full power was given to him in blessed Peter to rule, feed and govern the universal church by Jesus Christ our Lord; as is also contained in the acts of the general councils and in the sacred canons.

And since by the divine right of apostolic primacy the Roman pontiff is placed over the universal church, we further teach and declare that he is the supreme judge of the faithful, and that in all causes, the decision of which belongs to the church, recourse may be had to his tribunal, and that none may re-open the judgement of the apostolic see, than whose authority there is no greater, nor can any lawfully review its judgement. Wherefore they err from the right course who assert that it is lawful to appeal from the judgements of the Roman pontiffs to an ecumenical council, as to an authority higher than that of the Roman pontiff.'[31]

Words could hardly be plainer. There could be no appeal from a papal judgement. No person and no council could be permitted to review or modify the judgements of the Roman pontiffs. What purpose then was served by the council itself, or for that matter any future council? All that could be done was to rubber-stamp papal judgements. There was no room for compromise in the face of such claims. But the most stupendous pretension of all came in the fourth and last chapter 'Concerning the Infallible Teaching of the Roman Pontiff'.

'The first condition of salvation is to keep the rule of the true faith . . . in the apostolic see the Catholic religion and her holy and well-known doctrine has always been kept undefiled . . . This see of holy Peter remains ever free from all blemish of error . . .

'This gift, then, of truth and never-failing faith was conferred by heaven upon Peter and his successors in this chair, that they might perform their high office for the salvation of all . . .

'Therefore faithfully adhering to the tradition received from the beginning of the Christian faith, for the glory of God our Saviour, the exaltation of the Catholic religion, and the salvation of Christian people, the sacred council approving, we teach and define that it is a dogma divinely revealed: that the Roman pontiff, when he speaks *ex cathedra,* that is, when in discharge of the office of pastor and doctor of all Christians, by virtue of his supreme apostolic authority, he defines a doctrine regarding faith or morals to be held by the universal church, by the divine assistance promised to him in blessed Peter, is possessed of that infallibility with which the divine Redeemer willed that His church should be endowed for defining doctrine regarding faith or morals; and that therefore such definitions of the Roman pontiff are irreformable of themselves, and not from the consent of the church.

'But if anyone — which may God avert — presume to contradict this our definition — let him be anathema.'[32]

In certain respects, the content of this document represents a concise statement of what is the end result of the centuries-long development of the doctrine of papal power. What was implied a little earlier, that is, that there was no small degree of political machinations behind the scenes before the document was accepted and published, has reference primarily to this last point. But even here, it might be argued that papal infallibility is simply a logical necessity in the light of the other claims. Be this as it may, in defence of those who opposed it, the doctrine could hardly be considered a tradition handed down from the beginning of the Christian faith. Certainly, in no way did it satisfy the three criteria of the Vincentian Rule. It was definitely not supported by 'universality, antiquity and consent'. Even those most outspoken in its defence admitted that many had denied the doctrine.[33] In 1825, a British government commission had asked a panel of Irish Roman Catholic bishops whether it was held that the pope was infallible. They responded that it was not part of Catholic teaching. Gladstone, in his work dealing with Vatican Council I, cited a long list of historical examples reaching from 1661 to 1825 in which Roman Catholic prelates and scholars directly and openly repudiated the doctrine of papal infallibility. They did this even though they were well aware that others within their church held to the theory. One representative example of this attitude was Bishop Baines who in 1822 wrote, 'Bellarmine, and some other divines, chiefly Italians, have believed the pope infallible, when proposing *ex cathedra* an article of faith. But in England or Ireland I do not believe that any Catholic maintains the infallibility of the pope.'[34]

Hence, unless one argues with tongue in cheek, no valid case can be made for believing that the doctrine of papal infallibility was a matter accepted by the entire church in all places, and at all times.

How on earth then did such a doctrine come to be received by such an overwhelming margin? The case for the opposition had been presented with all the qualifications of the best scholarship. Urgings of practical expediency made little or no impact upon these men. They were concerned for truth. In spite of intolerable ridicule, some of them, like Bishop Strossmayer, stood their ground.[35] Others, such as the great Roman Catholic Church historian, Dr Dollinger, refused to be intimidated. Even sixteen years later, after being excommunicated and under ecclesiastical threats of eternal damnation, he reported in writing that he had studied the matter further, and that he had found that it was to an even greater extent than he had supposed based on a mass of fictions and forgeries.[36] Not only did such men oppose the doctrine, but many of them were persuaded that the council itself 'was neither legitimate in constitution, free in action, nor unanimous in doctrine'.[37] But the fact remains, even if historical research provides indisputable evidence of the grossest forms of behind-the-scenes Machiavellianism, a pope presiding over the council published the doctrine.

Thus 18 July 1870 marks a significant milestone in the theoretical development of papal power. That the doctrine was reconfirmed by later popes is evident in the following encyclicals: Pope Leo XIII, *Satis Cognitum* (1896); Pope Pius X, *Lamentabili* (1907); Pope Pius XII, *Mystici Corporis* (1943) and *Humani Generis* (1950). There can be absolutely no doubt about the intent of the decision of 18 July 1870.

When the pope speaks *ex cathedra,* in regard to doctrine, faith or morals, he is infallible. The doctrine dare not be misunderstood. It is stated in unequivocal terms. Anyone presuming to contradict it falls under a solemn anathema. How easy it would be to dwell on the implications of this doctrine at greater length, for surely no one is infallible but God Himself! Beside, all that is necessary to illustrate how fallacious is the doctrine is to show from the history of the popes themselves how many times they have been guilty of moral and doctrinal errors.[38] Such matters will be touched upon briefly in the concluding chapter, but we must first consider Vatican Council II, and its bearing upon the development of papal views of power.

According to Bishop Reuben H. Mueller, President of the National Council of the Church of Christ in the U.S.A., the Second Vatican Council was 'a new adventure in ecumenical co-operation' among the followers of the Lord Jesus Christ.[39] One of the cherished dreams of Pope John XXIII, who had called the council, was the reunion of all 'our brother Christians', the 'separated brethren'.[40] There can be little doubt, that in contrast with Vatican I, and with Trent, the overall tone of Vatican II appears to be quite moderate. The polemical tenor of those former councils is conspicuously absent. For readers who share the theological perspective of the Reformation, the documents contain not a few surprises. For example, there is a notable emphasis upon Holy Scripture. Also the council's 'master and pivotal document on the nature of the church'[41] would appear, at least to a superficial reader, to mitigate the pronouncements of Vatican I and of Trent, when it comes to the position and power of the pope. The fathers remain under the headship of 'the successor of Peter', but they share in the 'responsibility for the shepherding of the entire church of Christ'.[42] The very first document, *'Message to Humanity',* published by the fathers, while it was issued *'with the endorsement of the Supreme Pontiff'* had nevertheless been sent to the council by Pope John for discussion and 'amendment', if necessary.[43]

In spite of the general conciliatory tone of the no less than 103,014 words which make up the documents of Vatican II, the perceptive reader cannot fail to discern that there is in actuality little or no repudiation of Trent, or of Vatican I. If anything, when Trent or Vatican I are mentioned, the emphasis is never critical. Quite the contrary, Vatican II furthers 'the work begun by the Council of Trent', or follows 'in the footsteps of the First Vatican Council'.[44] In the third chapter of the *Dogmatic Constitution of the Church,* Peter is represented as being placed over the other apostles, and as being 'a permanent and visible source and foundation of unity of faith and fellowship'.[45] Then, following very closely in the footsteps of Vatican I, the reader is informed, 'And all this teaching about the institution, the perpetuity, the force and reason for the sacred primacy of the Roman pontiff and of his infallible teaching authority, this sacred synod again proposes to be firmly believed by all the faithful.'[46]

Should the reader fail to feel the full force of these words, there is ample reinforcement of their intent elsewhere. In the middle of Article 22 of Chapter 3, part of the decree reads that 'in virtue of his office, that is, as vicar of Christ and pastor of the whole church, the Roman pontiff has full, supreme and universal power over the church. And he can always exercise this power freely.'[47] The basis of this claim is, as in the past, that the 'Lord made Simon Peter alone the rock and key-bearer of the church (cf. Mt. 16:18–19)'.[48] In consequence, the position and power of the popes remains the same. Each pope possesses 'the prerogative of infallibility'.[49] His doctrinal definitions of faith and morals are 'irreformable'.[50] And, as it was concluded in Vatican I, so here also. The 'therefore', as it appears in the chain of argument, is unmistakable − that is, because of the pope's infallibility these doctrinal definitions 'need no approval of others, nor do they allow an appeal to any other judgement'.[51] Certainly, Pope Paul VI, who assumed the papal throne during the sessions of the council, was in full accord with these statements. In one of his first encyclical letters (*Ecclesiam Suam,* 6 August 1964) he wrote, 'We bear the responsibility of ruling the church of Christ because we hold the office of Bishop of Rome and consequently the office of successor to the blessed apostle Peter, the bearer of the master keys to the kingdom of God, vicar of the same Christ who made of him the supreme shepherd of His world-wide flock.'[52]

So then, notwithstanding the apparent pastoral tone and the cultivation of an ecumenical spirit, there can be little doubt that the documents of Vatican II follow in the traditions of Trent and of Vatican I. Even with regard to the question of infallibility, there is no significant modification. In case anyone might disagree on this score, he would be well advised to read Hans Kung's book *Infallible? An Enquiry*. As the title makes plain, Kung's main thesis is to subject the doctrine of infallibility to theological enquiry. What he has to say can hardly be misunderstood. He recognizes contrasting variations between Vatican I and II, but as touching infallibility, there is essential agreement.[53] The paradox in Kung's work is the antagonistic nature of his criticisms while he professes loyalty to the Roman Catholic Church. Out of a number of possible examples, the implications of the following are self-evident. Calling it his chief point, Kung writes 'That the greater the pope's efforts to take his teaching office seriously, the more they seem to take place at the expense of the credibility of that office and the inner cohesion of the church.' Later, he states categorically, 'The errors of the church's teaching office have been numerous and grave . . . they cannot be denied . . .'[54]

Kung's 'hot potato' merits much closer consideration than this brief mention. His intellectual ability and personal courage arouse the greatest admiration. But while he deserves the highest praise, there is no valid sense in which he can be viewed as representing the authoritative doctrinal position of the official Roman hierarchy. In fact, as this book was being prepared for publication, the Associated Press news release from Vatican City reported that Professor Kung had been removed from his teaching post, and that he could no longer be considered a bona fide theologian of the Roman Catholic

Church. Regardless of the incisive nature of his criticisms, Vatican II, together with Vatican I and the Tridentine Canons, must remain the final word on Roman Catholic doctrine. And as has been clearly seen, these councils, especially with regard to papal power, support unequivocally the whole Petrine theory. If there was any additional elucidation in theoretical development, it was with regard to the doctrine of papal infallibility. Vatican II, then, is where this discussion must stop. What remains is a critical evaluation of the theoretical foundations of the Petrine theory. This means that the relevant passages of Holy Scripture will be the primary area of discussion in the next chapter. This is only fitting, since scriptural arguments in support of the primacy and power of the Roman bishopric appeared incipiently as early as the fourth century, and continued right up till Vatican II.

NOTES

[1] Geoffrey Barraclough, *The Medieval Papacy* (London: Thames and Hudson, 1979), p. 196.
[2] Quoted in Preserved Smith, *The Age of the Reformation* (New York: Henry Holt and Company, 1930), p. 373.
[3] Francesco Guicciardini, trans., Sidney Alexander, *The History of Italy* (New York: The MacMillan Company, 1969), p. 433.
[4] Hubert Jedin, trans., Ernest Graf, *A History of the Council of Trent* (St Louis: B. Herder Book Company, 1957), I, 137.
[5] Smith, *op. cit.,* p. 381.
[6] Owen Chadwick, *The Reformation* (Baltimore: Penguin Books, 1966), p. 273.
[7] Henry S. Lucas, *The Renaissance and the Reformation* (New York: Harper and Brothers, 1934), p. 646.
[8] Chadwick, *op. cit.,* p. 273.
[9] Richard P. McBrien, *Catholicism* (2 vols; Minneapolis: Winston Press, Inc., 1980), II, 635.
[10] Philip Schaff, *History of the Christian Church* (AP & A n.d.) VIII, 279.
[11] Smith, *op. cit.,* p. 391.
[12] Henry Bettenson, *Documents of the Christian Church* (London: Oxford University Press, 1947), p. 374.
[13] *Ibid.,* p. 375.
[14] Trevor Gervase Jalland, *The Church and the Papacy* (London: SPCK, 1944), p. 454.
[15] James A. Corbett, *The Papacy, A Brief History* (New York: D. Van Nostrand Company, Inc., 1956), p. 59.
[16] Bettenson, *op. cit.,* p. 379.

[17] *Ibid.*

[18] One of the best studies in English dealing with the part played by Pius IX in the promulgation of the dogma of papal infallibility is that of J. B. Bury, *History of the Papacy in the 19th Century* (1864—1878), MacMillan and Co. Ltd., London, 1930.

[19] *Ibid.*, p. 50.

[20] *Ibid.*, p. 44.

[21] *Ibid.*, p. 60.

[22] As far as the 'railroading' of papal infallibility is concerned, together with the work of J. B. Bury, Geddes MacGregor's book, *The Vatican Revolution* (London: MacMillan & Co. Ltd., 1958) merits consideration.

[23] Bury, *op. cit.*, p. 92.

[24] Right Hon. W. E. Gladstone, M. P., *Rome and the Newest Fashions in Religion* (London: John Murray, 1875), XXXIV.

[25] *Ibid.*, p. 53.

[26] *Ibid.*, p. 54.

[27] Gertrude Himmelfarb, *Lord Acton, A Study in Conscience and Politics* (Chicago: 1952).

[28] Trevor Gervase Jalland, *The Church and the Papacy* (London: SPCK, 1944), p. 2.

[29] MacGregor, *op. cit.*, p. 169.

[30] *Ibid.*, p. 171.

[31] *Ibid.*, pp. 173, 175.

[32] *Ibid.*, pp. 175—179.

[33] MacGregor, *op. cit.*, p. 40.

[34] Gladstone, *op. cit.*, p. 48.

[35] See Appendix A.

[36] MacGregor, *op. cit.*, p. 70.

[37] John Emerich Edward Dalbert-Acton, *The History of Freedom and Other Essays* (New York: Books for Libraries Press, Inc., 1967), p. 550.

[38] Recommended on this subject is George Salmon, *The Infallibility of the Church* (London: John Murray, 1914).

[39] Walter M. Abbott S. J. Ed. *The Documents of Vatican II* (New York: Herder and Herder, 1966), xx.

[40] *Ibid.*, xx, 6.

[41] *Ibid.*, xv.

[42] *Ibid.*, xvi.

[43] *Ibid.*, pp. 1, 3.

[44] *Ibid.*, pp. 37, 456.

[45] *Ibid.*, p. 38.

[46] *Ibid.*

[47] *Ibid.*, p. 43.

[48] *Ibid.*

[49] *Ibid.*, p. 48.

[50] *Ibid.*, p. 49.

[51] *Ibid.*

[52] Pope Paul VI, *Ecclesiam Suam* (Boston, Mass., Vatican Translation, Daughters of St Paul), p. 5.

[53] Hans Kung, *Infallible? An Enquiry* trans. Erich Mosbacher (London: William Collins Sons & Co., Ltd., 1972), pp. 34, 56, 77, 102, *et al.*

[54] *Ibid.*, pp. 20, 27.

5
Holy Scripture and papal claims

As might readily be concluded from the preceding pages, papal claims have their roots in historical traditions laced together with the inferential interpretations of certain passages of Holy Scripture. Of course, from the point of view of the Roman church's authoritative pronouncements, the whole Petrine theory is viewed as nothing less than a Holy Spirit-inspired reflection of New Testament teaching. In this regard, not even the doctrine of papal infallibility would be exempted. However, as has been noted in the previous pages, not all Roman Catholic scholars have accepted these dogmatic assertions. Mention was made of men of the calibre of Karl Joseph van Hefele, Ignax Dollinger and Lord Acton. In the words of Lord Acton, papal infallibility was a doctrine unreachable by 'the weapon of human reason', a doctrine which 'resided in the inaccessible postulate rather than a demonstrable consequence of a system of religious faith'.[1] In more recent times, theologians such as Hans Kung have tried to point out that 'the case for the dogma of infallibility based on Scripture and tradition is plainly as meagre as it is brittle'.[2] Notwithstanding such weighty opinions, the documents of Vatican I and II seem to indicate that even infallibility derives from logical deductions based upon premises assumed to be the result of correct interpretations of Scripture. Certainly, no papal supporter would argue otherwise. Anyway, regardless of whether papal infallibility is found implicitly or explicitly in Scripture, what is certain is that Scripture does figure over and over again in papal claims and this in itself is sufficient justification to review the pertinent passages.

Without controversy, the first and the most important passage of Scripture upon which papal claims have been founded is Matthew 16:18: 'And I say also unto thee, That thou art Peter, and upon this rock I will build my church; and the gates of hell shall not prevail against it.'[3]

The statement was made after Peter had answered the question that the Lord Jesus had put to His disciples: 'But whom say ye that I am?' (Matthew 16:15.) Quite obviously, from the context, the answer to this question was of vital importance, for the truth contained therein was to form the foundation upon which the Lord was to build His church. Peter responded, 'Thou art the Christ, the Son of the living God.' The Lord 'then went on to say, 'Blessed art thou, Simon Barjona: for flesh and blood hath not revealed *it* unto thee, but my Father which is in heaven' (Matthew 16:16, 17). Then follow the words of verse 18, which literally could read: 'But I also say to thee, that thou art Peter (*petros,* a stone), and upon this the rock (*petra,* the rock), I will build my church (*ecclesia,* congregation), and the gates of hell shall not prevail against it.'

Viewing the words of Matthew 16:18 in context, the most natural interpretation seems to focus upon Peter's correct identification of the Son of man. Therefore, it is his confession of faith, when taken in its objective sense, which points to the rock. This would harmonize perfectly with other passages of Holy Scripture (e.g. Deut. 32:4, 18; 2 Sam. 22:2, 3, 32; 23:3). The church is thus infallible, that is, 'not liable to fail', because it is built upon the impregnable rock, that is, upon 'Christ, the Son of the living God'. Since it is built upon this rock 'the gates of hell' cannot prevail against it. How Peter could be such a rock is very difficult to imagine, for in the immediate context Peter is anything but infallible. Jesus Christ, the Son of the living God, had to say to him, 'Get thee behind me, Satan: thou art an offence unto me; for thou savourest not the things that be of God, but those that be of men' (Matthew 16:23).

From a comparison of other New Testament passages it is extremely difficult to conceive that Peter, or any of the apostles, had even the faintest knowledge of what is pretended in the Petrine theory. It must involve some very elaborate armchair gymnastics to prove from the Bible that the Lord Jesus appointed Peter to be the first pope, thus establishing the papal throne. If anything, the very fact that the Lord appointed twelve apostles is itself good reason to cast doubts upon the whole idea of one, and only one pope. As far as any throne was concerned, there were to be twelve, one for each of the apostles, but even this was to wait until the time when the kingdom of God would be established (Matthew 19:28).

It cannot be denied that Peter did manifest a comparative degree of prominence in the early chapters of The Acts of the Apostles, but such an admission hardly supports the Petrine theory. The very first chapter should point this out. It was not Peter who appointed Matthias to take the bishopric of Judas; it was all the disciples of Christ acting together in prayer and in casting lots (Acts 1:20–26). In chapter 2, Peter's apparent position of leadership seems to derive more from his force of character than from any special divine appointment. The same appears to be the case in the succeeding narrative right up to chapter 12. Then, with the words: 'And he went down from Judea to Caesarea, and there abode', Peter exits from the historical spotlight (Acts 12:19). The remaining sixteen chapters of this first history book of the spread of the gospel focus upon the ministry of Paul. Peter's one brief re-entry into the narrative in chapter 15 was primarily with a view to testifying in behalf of Paul's special apostleship to the Gentiles. Even after he spoke, the letters which were sent to the Christians in 'Antioch and Syria and Cilicia' were sent from 'the apostles and elders, with the whole church', not from Peter (Acts 15:23). There is not the slightest hint of any papal-like headship over any church. According to Paul, 'the household of God', meaning the 'congregation of God' is 'built upon the foundation of the apostles and prophets, Jesus Christ Himself being the chief corner-stone' (Ephesians 2:20). Also John, in the Revelation, describing the wall of the city of the heavenly Jerusalem, depicted it as having twelve foundations, each of which contains the names of the twelve apostles of the Lamb (Revelation 21:14). These references, and others such as 1 Corinthians 1:12; 15:5—11 and 2 Corinthians 11:5, 28 leave no room for a doctrine which teaches that Peter possessed sole authority over the corporate body of believers.

Peter himself, in his First Epistle left no indication that would lend credence to the Petrine theory. He identified himself as an apostle, not as the pope with ultimate authority over the people of God, and he left no doubt that Jesus Christ was the chief corner-stone of God's spiritual house (1 Peter 1:1; 2:5—8). Moreover, he classified himself as 'an elder' among others who were 'elders' (1 Peter 5:1). Further inferences along these lines can be found in The Gospel of Mark. Early tradition, such as Papias, asserted that Mark was both Peter's disciple and virtually his amanuensis in the composition of this second of the Synoptic Gospels. Strange that the Matthew 16:18 episode is not recounted in Mark, if Peter was indeed the rock upon which the Christian church would be built. Yet, even more, why does Mark record the incidents concerning which of the twelve was the greatest, and the request of James and John to sit on the right hand and on the left, if Peter had already been granted the position as the pope? (Mark 9:33—35; 10:35—45.)

There is also the account in Acts 15, where Peter manifested no papal prerogatives, and where, if anyone, James was the prominent spokesman. In this same connection, Galatians 2 describes Peter, along with James and John, as seeming to be a pillar in the church at Jerusalem. He is not even mentioned first. Beside this, he was withstood to the face, and publicly rebuked by Paul for his fearful indiscretions at Antioch (Acts 15; Galatians 2:9—14). Such references hardly fit into the general scheme of the Petrine theory. What seems more consistent with the overall teaching of Scripture is the view that the rock be related to Peter's confession: 'Thou art the Christ, the Son of the living God.' Here, more than anywhere, is the basic essential truth upon which the congregation of the Lord would be built, and nothing would prevail against such a solid infallible foundational rock. As Paul told the Corinthian Christians, 'For other foundation can no man lay than that is laid, which is Jesus Christ' (1 Corinthians 3:11).

Against all this, that is, against viewing Matthew 16:16—18 in the light of the New Testament as a whole, there yet remain the words which complete the response of the Lord Jesus to Peter's confession of faith. From the authoritative documents which make up the 'Magna Carta' of papal claims, it is obvious that they also figure prominently in the Petrine theory. The words appear in verse 19: 'And I will give unto thee the keys of the kingdom of heaven: and whatsoever thou shalt bind on earth shall be bound in heaven; and whatsoever thou shalt loose on earth shall be loosed in heaven.'

There is obviously a figurative meaning to such language. This is corroborated by other biblical passages (e.g. Isaiah 22: 22; Revelation 1:18; 3:7). Privilege and responsibility are clearly inherent in the possession and usage of such keys. Since the expression is modified by the phrase 'the kingdom of heaven', it apparently must be understood in close association with the significance of this phrase. Unto Peter were given privileges and responsibilities connected with the kingdom of heaven. Further expanded qualification states, 'And whatsoever thou shalt bind on earth shall be bound in heaven: and whatsoever thou shalt loose on earth shall be loosed in heaven.' Before jumping to any hasty conclusions, or attributing too much singularly to Peter, comparison of the context of Matthew 18:18 should be made. There the same privileges and responsibilities were extended to all the disciples of the Lord Jesus.[4]

The phrase 'the kingdom of heaven' is found thirty-three times in the Gospel of Matthew. A linguistic variation 'the kingdom of God' appears five times. There is really no essential difference between these two phrases, for where Matthew uses the one, the Gospels of Mark and Luke use the other. Matthew's distinctive preference for 'the kingdom of heaven' is apparently explainable by his intended readership. Since they were primarily Jewish, the substitution of the word 'heaven' for 'God' was an acceptable literary device. For example, the throne of heaven would mean the throne of God. In this same vein, an understanding of the historical context of the Gospel records helps to explain why the phrase is never adequately defined. Clearly implied in this phenomenon is the fact that no definition was ever needed, for the phrase obviously concerned something which was familiar to the Jews of that day. Their Holy Scriptures spoke of the time when the *God of Heaven* would set up *His kingdom* (Daniel 2:44; 7:14, 18, 27). Also, their Targums insert the phrase in contexts which leave no doubt that they expected to see an actual divine kingdom established on the earth (see Zechariah 14:9; Micah 4:7). Little wonder that we read in the Gospel of Mark of 'Joseph of Arimathaea, an honourable counsellor, which also waited for the kingdom of God' (Mark 15:43).

Anyone reading the Gospel narrative in an objective manner can hardly fail to notice the prominence given to the theme of the kingdom of God. Thoughtful attention to the actual subject material not only impresses this fact upon the mind, but also prepares the reader for a better appreciation of what the Lord intended by the words spoken to Peter in Matthew 16:18, 19. The Gospel record begins with the birth of the Lord Jesus Christ. He was of the house and lineage of King David. He was born to be 'King of the Jews' and 'a Governor that shall rule . . . Israel'. He was the long-promised Messiah born to sit upon 'the throne of his father David'. All of this had been predicted by the mouth of the holy prophets 'since the world began' (Matthew 1: 17, 20; 2:2, 6; Luke 1:30–33, 70; 2:11). His preaching, like that of John the Baptist, and the twelve apostles, had one main point: 'Repent; for the kingdom of heaven is at hand' (Matthew 3:2; 4:17; 10:7). His great 'sermon on the mount' was thoroughly permeated with an emphasis upon the divine kingdom (Matthew 5:3, 10, 19, 20; 6:10, 13, 33; 7:21). Apart from true repentance, and meeting the spiritual qualifications, there was no hope for entering the kingdom, even for those who had a prior claim through physical descendance from Abraham (Matthew 3:7–9; 8:11, 12; John 3:1–8). He chose twelve men as apostles, official representatives of His kingship, and they were promised the occupancy of twelve thrones ruling over the twelve tribes of Israel at the time of the inauguration of His kingdom (Matthew 19:28). They were given authoritative responsibilities commensurate with their exalted privileges, among which the words of Matthew 18:18, 19 have their setting. 'Verily I say unto you, whatsoever ye shall bind on earth shall be bound in heaven; and whatsoever ye shall loose on earth shall be loosed in heaven. Again I say unto you, that if two of you shall agree on earth as touching any thing that they shall ask, it shall be done for them of my Father which is in heaven.'

What the notion of this authoritative binding and loosing means can be gleaned from both biblical and contemporary rabbinical sources. John Lightfoot wrote of the possibility of producing thousands of examples of this particular concept from rabbinical writings. He asked, 'To think that Christ, when he used the common phrase, was not understood by his hearers in the common and vulgar sense, shall I call it a matter of laughter or of madness?'[5] From the examples cited from the school of Shammai, and from the school of Hillel, both of which were influential in the days of Christ, the meaning is quite clear. The phrase was used with reference to doctrines and judgements, and the idea of binding conveyed the meaning of forbidding and loosing signified permission. That such was indeed the intention may be inferred from such New Testament references as Matthew 13:52; 23:13; Luke 11:52. The last reference is particularly noteworthy for it connects the concept of 'the key of knowledge', that is, the truth concerning entrance into the kingdom of God. Peter and the other apostles were instructed in this matter, and they exercised their binding and loosing authority frequently throughout the early history of the book of Acts (see Acts 2:37–47; 3:1–26; 4:1–12; 5:17–32; 15:1–29; 21:17–26).

One interesting footnote with regard to the exercise of the

divine knowledge granted to Peter and the other apostles comes out when closer attention is paid to the verbal construction in Matthew 16:19; 18:18. For those not familiar with Greek, any good interlinear version should serve to bring out what is highly noteworthy. To borrow from the literal English translation of Alfred Marshall, the pertinent part is rendered: 'Whatever thou bindest on the earth shall be having been bound in the heavens, and whatever thou loosest on the earth shall be having been loosed in the heavens.' Matthew 18:18, other than being in the plural form, could be rendered in the same way. Keeping in mind that binding means 'to forbid', and loosing means 'to permit'; also that the exercise concerns doctrinal judgements, the interpretation of the words seems quite clear. Whatever the apostles were forbidding or permitting, they were doing so because it had already been forbidden or permitted in heaven. In simple terms, their teaching reflected the principles of the kingdom of heaven. They were a very special group of people, the foundation of the household of God, called out of darkness into God's marvellous light, entrusted with the oracles of God, and thus, because of their privileges, they were able to make known the will of God. C. B. Williams has rendered these two verses as follows: 'I will give you the keys of the kingdom of heaven, and whatever you forbid on earth must be what is already forbidden in heaven, and whatever you permit on earth must be what is already permitted in heaven.

'I solemnly say to you, whatever you forbid on earth must be already forbidden in heaven, and whatever you permit on earth must be already permitted in heaven.'[6]

While we are touching upon the verbal construction of these verses, this might be a good place to mention the words recorded in John 20:23: 'Whose soever sins ye remit, they are remitted unto them; and whose soever sins ye retain, they are retained.' This verse, along with the two passages in Matthew, has been used to provide scriptural sanction for the sacerdotalism of the Roman church. However, the perfect tense, when rendered correctly, prohibits any concept of men being able to forgive sins on behalf of God. When translated literally John 20:23 could read as follows: 'Whose soever sins ye forgive (aorist, active, subjunctive), they have been forgiven (perfect, passive, indicative): whose soever sins ye retain, they have been retained' (tenses correspond as before). Clearly, the basic intent is akin to that in the Matthew passages. In simple terms, the Lord taught the disciples to treat as forgiven those who were already forgiven by God. Such a paraphrase gives the Greek perfect tense its full grammatical force, namely the idea of the continuance of completed action.[7]

Understanding John 20:23 and the verses in Matthew as suggested makes the exercise of 'the keys of the kingdom' much easier to appreciate. It also makes papal pretensions all the more ludicrous. The apostles were elevated to the rank and privilege enjoyed by the scribes, but they were not to perpetuate the abuses of the scribes. They were to teach the Word of God and not to make substitutions taken from the doctrines and commandments of men (Mark 7:1—13). They were not to exceed their authority. They were interpreters of God's Word, and as such they were to persuade men to do the will of God on earth as it was done in heaven (Matthew 6:10). No pope, no priest, or no man for that matter, can go beyond this commission. What sheer arrogant nonsense for any human ecclesiastical authority to pretend that, through its own power or holiness, it can determine who enters, or who does not enter, the kingdom of God! Apart from meeting the conditions established by God Himself, and so clearly set forth in His Word, it is wasted breath for any man to claim the power to forgive sins. Yea, worse, it is blasphemy! 'Who can forgive sins but God only?' (Mark 2:7—12). Paul warned the Corinthian Christians 'not to think of men above that which is written', and Peter wrote to the Christians in Asia Minor to speak according to 'the oracles of God' (1 Corinthians 4:6; 1 Peter 4:11).

Beside Matthew 16:16—19, there are probably two other passages in Holy Scripture that ought to be mentioned in relation to papal claims. They are John 21:15—17, and

Luke 22:32. John Henry Newman is quoted as saying that 'The long history of the contest for or against the pope's infallibility has been but a growing insight into the meaning of these three texts.'[8] The reader, of course, must study these texts for himself, but it surely involves some fancy exegetical footwork (hardly 'growing insight') to interpret them as teaching the conferral upon Peter of absolute episcopal jurisdiction over the other apostles, and over the whole church. The words of John 21:15–17: 'Feed my lambs . . . feed my sheep,' when viewed in context, describe a special renewal of Peter's apostleship after the humiliation of his threefold shameful denial of his Lord (John 18:15–27). They do imply a teaching ministry, but then the other apostles were also commissioned to go and 'teach all nations' (Matthew 28:19). As far as Luke 22:32 is concerned, the context once again bears consideration. At least, it makes it very clear that Peter was no infallible rock (cf. vv. 33, 34). The Lord forewarned Peter that he would be guilty of denying Him three times. Therefore, the Lord uttered words suited to encourage Peter, certainly not to appoint him as exalted infallible head over the other apostles.

What more can be said on this subject? Each reader must think carefully about the whole matter for himself. If the Lord Jesus Christ had intended to establish the supreme authority of Peter, and to have that authority perpetuated in the bishops at Rome, then it is only reasonable to assume that He would have distinctly informed His followers. So important an office would surely have been mentioned in the clearest of terms. Other sacred offices are set forth in Holy Scripture, yet strange silence prevails with regard to that which would be the highest of all. There is not one jot or tittle, anywhere from Genesis to Revelation, about any man being a regal-sacerdotal king, who as vicegerent of Christ rules over the visible church upon the earth. Such a thing just cannot be found in Holy Scripture. From whence then does it come? In the light of what has been set forth in the preceding pages, only one answer seems plausible. It is that which the Lord Jesus Christ and both Peter and Paul inveighed against, namely, '*the tradition of men*' (Matthew 15:1—9; Mark 7: 9—13; Colossians 2:8; 1 Peter 1:18). As it was with the Jews in the Old Testament dispensation, so it was with the church of Rome under the New; both elevated their man-made traditions above the written Word of God. If the Lord condemned the former, would He not have condemned the latter? Men have not changed, be they Jew or Gentile. The warnings of Scripture are as valid today as when they were first written.

'Beware lest any man spoil you through philosophy and vain deceit, after the tradition of men, after the rudiments of the world, and not after Christ.'

NOTES

[1] John Emerich Edward Dalberg-Acton, *The History of Freedom and Other Essays* (New York: Books for Libraries Press, Inc., 1967), p. 512.

[2] Hans Kung, *Infallible? An Enquiry* trans. Erich Mosbacker (London: William Collins Sons & Co., Ltd., 1972), p. 99.

[3] Pope John Paul II, in his first public speech made on the ceremonial occasion of his coronation (Vatican City, 22 October 1978), reaffirmed unapologetically the claims of papal authority and the Petrine theory. He referred to the confession of Peter and the words of Matthew 16:16—18 and said, 'The churchly aspect of the people of God draws its origins, is born indeed by the words of faith, and is bound to the man who pronounced them. You are Peter — rock, stone — and upon you, as upon a rock, I will build My church.'

[4] The Documents of Vatican II Chap. III Art. 22 acknowledge this fact. However, there is a significant qualification. This power was granted 'to the college of apostles, joined with their head (Mt. 18:18; 28:16—20)'.

[5] John Lightfoot, *Hebrew and Talmudical Exercitations* (Oxford: University Press, 1859), pp. 234—240.

[6] Charles B. Williams, *The New Testament, A Translation in the Language of the People* (Chicago: Moody Press, 1950), pp. 47, 51.

[7] A. T. Robertson, *A Grammar of the Greek New Testament* (New York: Hodder & Stoughton, 1915), p. 893.

[8] John Schulte, *Roman Catholicism, Old and New from the Standpoint of the Infallibility Doctrine* (Toronto: Belford Brothers, 1876), p. 311.

Conclusion

Jaroslav Pelikan, borrowing from Sir Winston Churchill's description of the Soviet Union, called the Roman church 'a riddle wrapped in a mystery inside an enigma'.[1] The words appropriately summarize my sentiments with regard to the Roman papacy. In broad outline, the historical origins of papal power reach back to as early as the fourth century. The theoretical and practical development of that power extends over the centuries which followed, all the way till the twentieth century. The authority of the Bishop of Rome progressed from the diocese of his own city, where it had definite limits, to that of universal bishop over the whole earth. At times, particularly during the Middle Ages, papal power became virtually a super-power without equal even in temporal matters. Yet, all along, its foundational claims were supposedly spiritual in nature.

I use the word 'supposedly' because it seems apparent that in the transitional developments of papal power there was an insidious shift of emphasis. Without realizing what was happening, the church lost the dynamic of its spiritual power in exchange for a mess of political pottage. The nature of the change was gradual, probably having its roots in the circumstances and consequences surrounding the decline and fall of the Roman Empire. On a much smaller scale similar developments have been witnessed many times throughout the history of Christianity. Ecclesiastical organizations are governed by fallible men, and as Lord Acton so laconically put it, 'Power corrupts, and absolute power corrupts absolutely.' Running together with this recurrent

108

tendency, there is the subtle process wherein a militant movement loses its vitality because loyalty switches inconspicuously from its ideals to its institutions.

Perhaps the spirit of this process can be illustrated by the fable of the dog which lost its bone by grabbing for what it thought was a bigger bone. What happened was that the dog came to the side of a pond and there, looking down, saw reflected on the surface of the water a dog holding a bone in its mouth. The imaginary bone looked much bigger and better. So it let go of the one it had in order to grasp at the one it thought was better. The moral is obvious. In reaching for temporal and political power, the papacy lost its control over the primary ministry of the church, that is, the spiritual dynamic of the gospel remained no longer at the centre of its *raison d'être*. Maybe this is what Dante had in mind when in the nineteenth canto of his *Inferno* he wrote,

> Ahi! Constantin, di quanto mal fu matre,
> Non la tua conversion, ma qualla dote
> Che da te prese il primo ricco patre!

> Alas! Constantine, how much misfortune you caused,
> Not by becoming Christian, but by that dowry
> Which the first rich father accepted from you![2]

Of course, the institutionalized papacy of the Middle Ages could hardly be expected to view itself as being caught in the interplay of historical forces which produced radical changes in its structure and ministry. On the contrary, the inherent bias was to view its origins and development as being the practical outworking of divine doctrinal concepts. Such doctrines, as my research has indicated, were themselves subject to development and systematization. They originated supposedly in the teachings of Holy Scripture, with Matthew 16:18, 19 being the chief corner-stone. Building upon inferences from this passage, champions of papal pretensions bolstered their claims by subtle arguments, and by the use of cleverly fabricated forgeries. Essentially, the end result was the Petrine theory which was eventually fitted with the supreme capstone of papal infallibility. This meant that according to official Roman Catholic dogma, the pope is nothing less than God's vicegerent on earth, who when speaking *ex cathedra* on matters dealing with faith and morals, is under the direct infallible control of the Holy Spirit.

Having summarized very briefly the scope of my findings, there are two things I would like to do before concluding: (1) raise the question of the truthfulness of papal claims; and (2) touch upon the historical facts which show that popes have erred. Of course, both points are self-evidently related. With regard to the first one, I readily admit that discussion might not be as simple as it seems. However, it cannot be shelved for a number of reasons. In my case, these reasons stem primarily from a personal bent of mind which functions in a framework where objective Christian truth is very important. I believe whole-heartedly that the Christianity taught in the Holy Scriptures is true. Such a belief produces a reflex reaction which causes me to question any form of Christianity which goes beyond what is written in Holy Scripture. That the papal claims do go beyond Scripture cannot be denied. Herein lies the difficulty in testing the truthfulness of papal claims. For one thing, it involves an excursion into a sort of forbidden no man's land between history and theology. This, in turn, leads to a frustrating experiment in attempting to 'unscrew' the inscrutable. I know that this must sound somewhat facetious but, in reality, the quest does indeed lead very early to a basic fallacy in logic known as 'circular reasoning'. Let me try to explain. From the Roman Catholic point of view, the truthfulness of papal claims rests upon the authority of papal claims. Stated differently, papal claims are held to be true, because papal authority claims that they are true. In this context, further discussion is obviously useless. All reasonable argument is thus stalemated. Only an existential blind leap of faith, or what some neo-orthodox theologians call a divine-human-encounter-experience of revelation can make sense in the face of such a logical impasse.

Sometimes it is argued that the preceding deadlock can be terminated simply by recognizing that the Roman church is older than other churches. Even if such a claim were historically true, which it is not, there still remains an enormous chasm to cross before arriving at the Petrine theory. From The Acts of the Apostles we learn that there were in existence many churches which antedated the founding of a church at Rome. Moreover, such a line of argument would lead to the church at Jerusalem being the oldest church (cf. Acts 2:47). What would this prove? The prominence and prestige of the Roman church came not because it was the earliest of the churches. There were churches established in Greece before there were in Italy. Does this prove that the Greek Orthodox Church was earlier than the Roman church? From a strictly historical perspective they had simultaneous and mingled origins. Like a flowing stream which strikes a rock and divides, neither resultant can claim to be the exclusive original. A similar problem prevails even with regard to Luther and Calvin. To argue that they are the founders of the evangelical tradition is as ridiculous as if one were to argue that the American ideal of government began with the protest against Nazism. The essential question cannot be resolved as long as there persists circular argument. If papal claims depend upon papal authority, then discussion is vain. Without Holy Scripture as the final court of appeal, there is no resolution.

The second point, regarding the question of papal errors, is not as abstruse as the first one. If it were, then Hans Kung would hardly have written, 'The errors of the church's teaching office have been numerous and grave . . .'[3] Apparently, they are of such a nature that he could refer to them as 'the classical errors now widely admitted . . .'.[4] Again, I find these statements to be dumbfounding. It is not that I would disagree with them. On the contrary, I would agree, but they are made by one who considers himself loyal to the Roman Catholic Church, and yet who makes statements which fly right into the face of the authoritative definitions of Roman Catholic dogma. According to the Tridentine Canons,

Vatican I and Vatican II, the Roman church not only professes to be the one true church, but also postulates that 'In
the apostolic see the Catholic religion and her holy and well-
known doctrine has always been kept undefiled . . . ever free
from all blemish or error . . .'[5] What is more, it is clearly
stated that from this teaching, 'no one can deviate without
loss of faith and of salvation'.[6] Talk about a dilemma! Kung
tells his readers that 'It is impossible honestly to deny objective errors committed by the church's teaching office both
ordinary and extraordinary,'[7] and yet, the church's teaching
office personified in the popes claims freedom from all
blemish and error. Moreover, anyone contradicting this
doctrine puts himself immediately under a solemn anathema.

Let the reader grasp the weight of the dilemma. In the
final analysis, there is no escaping the conclusion that submission to the Roman church must rest upon an act of
private judgement. But how can anyone submit, if the papacy
has indeed been guilty of 'extraordinary' errors? By way of a
few examples, take first the case of Pope Liberius (358): not
only did he subscribe to a heretical Arian creed, but he
anathematized Athanasius, the great defender of the Nicene
Creed. Also Pope Zozimus (417—418) first pronounced
Pelagius to be orthodox, and then reversed his judgement.
Then there was Honorius (625—638) who was condemned
as a heretic by both a council and by several subsequent
popes. There was the case of Hadrian II (867—872) declaring
civil marriages to be valid, and then Pius VII (1800—1823)
condemning them as invalid. Along similar lines, Eugene IV
(1431—1447) condemned Joan of Arc to be burned alive
as a witch, while Benedict XV in 1919 declared her to be a
saint. The suppression and the restoration of the Jesuits were
both brought to pass by papal decrees. The recommendation
and the condemnation of Bible reading likewise fell under
papal pronunciamentos.

One of the more notorious examples of extraordinary,
and it might be added, shameful erroneous actions of the
papal Curia was the condemnation of Galileo. The Sacred
Congregation of the Holy Office, created in 1542, had the

authority to ban books judged harmful to the faith and morals of communicants. The catalogue of books known as the *Index of Prohibited Books* waged war on the Copernican theory for over two centuries. The *Index* of 1704 even contained the prohibition against 'all books that teach the mobility of the earth or the immobility of the sun'.[8] Anyone who has made a serious attempt to look at this side of papal power can scarcely charge Kung with exaggeration when he declares that, 'In every century the errors of the church's teaching office have been numerous and indisputable . . .'[9] Dilemma indeed! Beside these historical examples, which could be expanded to fill many pages, what of the gross wickednesses, intrigues and immoralities of many of the popes?[10] I prefer to omit discussion of this side of papal history. Reliable works are readily available for the interested reader. I have said enough. What remains is my bewilderment. How, in the face of undeniable and indisputable historical facts, can any sane and sensible person make that act of private judgement (surely only by some form of intellectual suicide) wherein he submits to what the Roman church teaches concerning papal power?

This rather vehemently worded question might provide a convenient exit to end this study. Little can be gained by a further multiplication of words. Besides, I have accomplished my objective. After thousands of pages of research, I have arrived at answers which satisfactorily have enabled me to cross the gap between the simple straightforward teachings of Holy Scripture and the *de facto* power of the hierarchical body which governs the Roman church. However, in concluding, let me borrow and adapt a somewhat far-out imaginary parable which should serve to summarize my overall sentiments. In order to get the point across with greater force, let me personalize the parable, and let me revert to the setting of being a kind of tour leader in and around Vatican City.

Just suppose that while I am leading my small party around the magnificent splendours of Vatican City, an uninvited odd-looking creature attaches himself to our group.

In spite of his nondescript features, he is polite, and explains that he is making some exploratory inquiries concerning famous places on Planet Earth. He makes it very clear that he will be no trouble, and that he will not be with us long, for he has a spaceship hovering outside waiting to whisk him away to his next appointment. All he really wants, so he informs us, is to know the real meaning and the essential significance of the buildings, the statues and the activities of the multitudes of people which surround us. At that point, a passer-by, who had been struck by the odd appearance of our extra-terrestrial visitor, and who had stopped to listen to what he had to say, intrudes into the conversation. Gesturing with an all-encompassing sweep of his hand, and with reassuring candour, he blurts out, 'This is the Christian religion.' Then, continuing, he exclaims that all that is really needed to find an adequate explanation of what it all signifies is a copy of the New Testament, which can be obtained in the authorized tourist shop across the square.

Not being the kind of alien to waste time, he allows his computer-like brain to make one further sweep of the surroundings, expresses his appreciation, exits with amazing speed through the main doors, visits the tourist shop, picks up a copy of the New Testament, and within seconds is back at the controls of his saucer-like spacecraft. After blast off, he begins to feed the data from his observations into the central information bank, and acting on the word of the earthlings, with a view to registering an explanatory summarization of his visit, he files the facts taken from the New Testament into the terminal marked Comparative Analysis. Curious concerning the results, he pushes the print-out button, and after a few bleeps and blurps a message appears on the screen: RELATIONSHIP — IF — ANY — REMOTE — POSSIBLE — HUMAN — ERROR — INSERTION — OF — WRONG — BOOK.

True enough, the space-travelling visitor is imaginary, but as mentioned, he was introduced by way of analogy simply to highlight my own sentiments over the great disparate gap between what attaches to the ecclesiastical colossus headed by the papacy at Rome, and that which the New Testament can support. Nevertheless, somehow or other, I was determined to make an attempt to bridge the gap. In certain respects, I never lost my bewilderment, for the deeper my research took me, and the farther I was removed from the days of the New Testament apostles, the more shaky became the bridge. Particularly was this the case as I wandered around in the no man's land between theology and history during the Middle Ages. However, among the political and religious vicissitudes of that period, I was able to discover sufficient landmarks to keep me headed in the right direction. And it was there, more than anywhere, that I began to comprehend both the theoretical foundations and the actual historical forces which shaped the development of papal power. I had one great advantage over our imaginary space traveller. I had more data than he had. Naturally, as can readily be expected, that can make a world of difference as far as drawing the right conclusions is concerned. Should he ever return, perhaps he might happen upon someone who could share with him a few excerpts from this study which, when fed into his computer, might possibly print out: REMOTE RELATIONSHIP – TIME + HISTORICAL FORCES = RADICAL TRANSFORMATION – RESULT = HYBRID RELIGION.

NOTES

[1] Jaroslav Pelikan, *The Riddle of Roman Catholicism* (New York: Abingdon Press, 1959), p. 13.
[2] Dante Aleghieri, *La Divina Commedia* (Milano: Tipografia Editoriale Lucchi, 1959), p. 125.
[3] Hans Kung, *Infallible? An Enquiry* trans. Erich Mosbacher (London: William Collins Sons & Co., Ltd., 1971), p. 27.
[4] *Ibid.*
[5] Geddes MacGregor, *op. cit.*, pp. 175–179.
[6] *Ibid.*, pp. 173, 175.
[7] Kung, *op. cit.*, p. 144.
[8] George Salmon, *The Infallibility of the Church* (London: George Murray, 1914), p. 237. A good guide to the history of prohibitory indexes is the work by George Haven Putnam, *The Censorship of the Church of Rome*, 2 vols (New York: G. P. Putman's Sons, 1907).
[9] Kung, *op. cit.*, p. 28. Kung, of course, cites many examples to support this

assertion. There are other works which deal particularly in greater detail with this matter — e.g. Loraine Boettner, *Roman Catholicism* (Philadelphia: The Presbyterian and Reformed Publishing Company, 1964).

[10] The reader need not look in Protestant 'anti-Catholic' books for a detailed account of this aspect of papal history. It is described with surprising frankness in a book displaying the Imprimatur of Cardinal Spellman: Glen D. Kittler, *The Papal Princes* (New York: Funk & Wagnalls, 1960).

Appendix
The First Vatican Council:
papal infallibility

Listed among the opponents of the definition of papal infallibility at the First Vatican Council were some of the most scholarly and cultured prelates of that day, such as Dupanloup, Darboy, Hefele, Kenrick, Ketteler, Maret, Rauscher, Schwarzenberg and Strossmayer. To these could be added historians and writers such as Dollinger, Gratry, Montalembert and Lord Acton. It reflects an extreme bias indeed to dismiss the arguments of the opposition under the catch-all word 'inopportuneness'. Yes, there were many at the council who did argue that the definition should be delayed because it would widen the gap between the Roman Catholic Church and the modern world, but there were a notable number that rested their case solidly on historical and biblical grounds. And on such grounds, as Bishop Hefele protested, 'The question was not one of being opportune or inopportune; infallibility was simply not true.'[1]

One of the most outspoken opponents of the doctrine of papal infallibility was Josef Strossmayer. J. B. Bury, who succeeded Lord Acton as the Regius Professor of Modern History at Cambridge University, called him 'the most courageous man at Rome'.[2] James Cardinal Gibbons, himself a participant at the council, described him as 'the most eloquent prelate of the council'.[3] His scholarship was self-evident, and in spite of denigrating stories about his personal life which some of his opponents were wont to spread abroad, his character was irreproachable.

He was a man who did not mince words. Several of the turbulent scenes that disturbed the peace of the council were due to his speeches. In one debate he spoke out for reform, not only in the College of Cardinals, but also in the see of St Peter itself. He went as far as to call the canon law 'that confusion of Babel', and he made no secret of his disapproval of the abuse which the infallibilists made of quotations from the Bible. In another speech, when he tried to counter anti-Protestant generalizations which had been presented in the introduction to the schema ' Of the faith', he was interrupted by the president of the council and told that 'This is not the place to praise Protestants.' His manner had been courteous, but he had dared to declare that the judgement against the Protestants was consistent 'neither with truth or charity'.

As this particular speech continued, he was met with angry shouts from various sides of the assembly: 'Shame, shame, down with the heretic.' Others, infuriated by his words, muttered such sentiments as: 'He is Lucifer, anathema, anathema,' and 'He is another Lucifer, let him be cast out.' When Mgr Place, Bishop of Marseilles, spoke up and said, 'I do not condemn you,' he was met with the response: 'All of us, all of us condemn him!'

Obviously, there was more behind such outbursts than the mere question of misrepresenting Protestantism. Strossmayer had become a marked man. His leadership among the anti-infallibilists was common knowledge. In this same speech he had dared to criticize the restrictions which shackled the order of procedure, and also to condemn the principle that propositions of faith could be decided by counting noses. A majority of votes, in his mind, was no way to determine doctrine which would 'bind the conscience of the Catholic world on condition of eternal life and death'.[4] In his opinion the council lacked both liberty and truth. He was not alone in this opinion. Others, such as Archbishop Kenrick, said virtually the same thing. Kenrick, according to Gibbons, 'was violently opposed to the definition, not only because he considered its inopportuneness, but because he did not see that it was part of the deposit of faith...'[5]

Besides Kenrick's spoken words during the council, we have the complete seventy-five page text of speech which he had intended but was unable to give, due to a sudden unexpected shutting off of the debate. In spite of the rules which forbid the printing of speeches under severe penalties, he nevertheless, in his own words, 'deemed best that his divine right of expressing his views on this momentous business to his fellow-bishops, and to others who are entitled to an interest in the council, should be exercised through the press'.[6] After setting forth biblical and historical arguments in opposition to the doctrine of papal infallibility, he concluded by making reference to 'trickery' which stacked the deck in favour of those who were determined to exalt the authority of the pope.[7] In Hans Kung's words, 'As painful and embarrassing as it may be to admit, this council resembled a well organized and manipulated totalitarian congress rather than a free gathering of free Christian people.'[8]

'Trickery' might be judged too prejudicial a word, but the papal bull *Multiplices inter,* which became the parliamentary handbook for the council, was clearly on the side of the infallibilists. For example, only the pope had the initiative to propose topics and only he possessed the prerogative to nominate the officers of the council. Add to this the predisposition of loyalty which the prelates felt towards the pope as the head of the Roman Catholic Church and it becomes easier to understand why the questions of liberty and truth could be overlooked and how debate could drift to the soft-ground of inopportunism, or inexpediency.

In Lord Acton's words, the result was that the majority came to a mind-set which was 'acting less from conviction than by command'.[9] Or, as he wrote in another place, 'Authority must conquer history.'[10] What Acton meant, of course, as Bishop Hefele had so frankly stated during the debates, was that no genuine historical document could be found which implied that the ancient church had believed in the pope's infallibility. Bishop Richard V. Whelan described this mind-set in a letter he wrote to Bishop Dupanloup: 'I am convinced that all the arguments which can be accumulated will have no effect with those who favour this doctrine. In one way or another they reject everything. Reasons mean nothing. Facts count for nothing... They want it; they have decided on it; nothing can prevent it (humanly).'[11]

Another speech which summarized the biblical and historical arguments appeared under the name of Bishop Strossmayer in an Italian translation printed in Florence shortly after the council adjourned. Before long translations appeared also in Germany, South America and even in Strossmayer's native land. An English translation was reported in the *Guardian* of 28 June 1871. It bore the title: 'The speech of Bishop Strossmayer on the infallibility of the pope, delivered before the late Ecumenical Council in Rome.' Even today the speech continues to be distributed under Strossmayer's name. It was published as recently as 1967 in Belgrade, Yugoslavia, in a book containing a selection of famous speeches. Evidently, while the content reveals familiarity with the leading personalities at the council, and with the arguments both pro and con, its genuineness is open to question. According to one writer, the real author was an obscure Mexican friar named Jose Augustin de Escudero.[12]

This dispute over authorship has had the negative effect of discrediting the value of the tract itself. As was mentioned in earlier pages, forged documents played a significant part, not only in the development of papal power but also in the arguments used by the supporters of papal infallibility.[13] But most of these forgeries were palmed off as authoritative legal documents. If this tract be a forgery it does not fall into this category. It was simply a condensation of arguments, not based on questions of expediency or inexpediency, but on the main question of whether or not the doctrine of papal infallibility could stand the critical test of history and Scripture. It is with this in mind that the tract is included in this appendix.

An English translation of the Italian text of a speech published at Florence in 1870 under the name of Bishop Joseph Strossmayer

Venerable fathers and brethren – It is not without trembling, yet with a conscience free and tranquil before God who lives and sees me, that I open my mouth in the midst of you in this august assembly. From the time that I have been sitting here with you, I have followed with attention the speeches that have been made in the hall, hoping with great desire that a ray of light descending from on high might enlighten the eyes of my understanding, and permit me to vote the canons of this holy ecumenical council with perfect knowledge of the case.

Penetrated with the feelings of responsibility, of which God will demand of me an account, I have set myself to study with the most serious attention the Old and New Testaments, and I have asked these venerable monuments of truth to make known to me if the holy pontiff, who presides here, is truly the successor of St Peter, vicar of Jesus Christ, and the infallible doctor of the church. To resolve this grave question I have been obliged to ignore the present state of things, and to transport myself in mind, with the evangelical torch in my hand, to the days when there was neither Ultramontanism nor Gallicanism, and in which the church had for doctors St Paul, St Peter, St James and St John – doctors to whom no one can deny the divine authority without putting in doubt that which the holy Bible, which is here before me, teaches us, and which the Council of Trent has proclaimed as the rule of faith and of morals. I have then opened these sacred pages. Well (shall I dare to say it?), I have found nothing either near nor far which sanctions the opinion of the Ultramontanes. And still more, to my very great surprise, I find in the apostolic days no question of a pope, successor to St Peter, and vicar of Jesus Christ, any more than of Mahomet who did not then exist. You, Monsignor Manning, will say that I blaspheme; you, Monsignor Fie, that I am mad. No, Monsignori, I do not blaspheme, and I am not mad. Now, having read the whole New Testament, I declare before God, with my hand raised to that great crucifix, that I have found no trace of the papacy as it exists at this moment. Do not refuse me your attention, my venerable brethren, and with your murmuring and interruptions do not justify those who say, like Father Hyacinthe, that this council is nothing, but that our votes have been from the beginning dictated by authority. If such were the case, this august assembly, on which the eyes of the whole world are turned, would fall into the most shameful discredit. If we wish to make it great, we must be free. I thank his Excellency, Monsignor Dupanloup, for the sign of approbation which he makes with his head: this gives me courage, and I go on.

Reading then the sacred books with the attention with which the Lord has made me capable, I do not find one single chapter, or one little verse, in which Jesus Christ gives to St Peter the mastery over the apostles, his fellow workers. If Simon, son of Jonas, had been what we believe his holiness Pius IX to be today, it is wonderful that He had not said to him, 'When I have ascended to My Father, you should all obey Simon Peter as you obey Me. I establish him My vicar upon earth.'

Not only is Christ silent on this point but so little does He think of giving a head to the church, that when He promises to His apostles to judge the twelve tribes of Israel (Matt. 19:28), He promises them twelve thrones, one for each, without saying that among those thrones one shall be higher than the others – which shall belong to Peter. Certainly, if He had wished that it should be so, He would have said it. What do we conclude from this sentence? Logic tells us that Christ did not wish to make St Peter the head of the apostolic college. When Christ sent the apostles to conquer the world, to all He gave the promise of the Holy Spirit. Permit me to repeat it: if He had wished to constitute Peter His vicar, He would have given him the chief command over His spiritual army. Christ – so says the Holy Scripture -- forbade Peter and his colleagues to reign or to exercise lordship, or to have authority over the faithful like the kings of the Gentiles (Luke 22:25). If St Peter had been elected pope, Jesus would not have spoken thus; but according to our tradition, the papacy holds in its hands two swords, symbols of spiritual and temporal power.

One thing has surprised me very much. Turning it over in my mind, I said to myself, 'If Peter had been elected pope, would his colleagues have been permitted to send him with St John to Samaria to announce the gospel of the Son of God?' What do you think, venerable brethren, if at this moment we permitted ourselves to send his Holiness Pius IX and his Excellency Mons. Plantier to go to the Patriarch of Constantinople, to pledge him to put an end to the Eastern schism?

But here is another still more important fact. An ecumenical council is assembled at Jerusalem to decide on the questions which divide the faithful. Who would have called together this council if St Peter had been pope? St Peter. Who would have presided at it? St Peter or his legate. Who would have promulgated the canons? St Peter. Well, nothing of this occurred. The apostle assisted at the council as all the others did, yet it was not he who summed up, but St James; and when the decrees were promulgated, it was in the name of the apostles, the elders and the brethren (Acts 15). Is it thus that we do in our church? The more I examine, O venerable brethren, the more I am convinced that in the Scriptures the son of Jonas does not appear to be first.

Now, while we teach that the church is built upon St Peter, St Paul (whose authority cannot be doubted) says, in his epistle to the Ephesians 2:20, it is built on the foundation of the apostles and prophets, Jesus Christ Himself being the chief corner-stone. And the same apostle believes so little in the supremacy of St Peter, that he openly blames those who would say, 'We are of Paul; we are of Apollos' (1 Cor. 1:12), as those who say, 'We are of Peter.' If therefore this last apostle had been the vicar of Christ, St Paul would have taken great care not to censure so violently those who belonged to his own colleagues. The same apostle, counting up the offices of the church, mentions apostles, prophets, evangelists, doctors and pastors. Is it to be believed, my venerable brethren, that St Paul, the great apostle of the Gentiles, would have forgotten the first of these offices, the papacy, if the papacy had been of divine institution? The forgetfulness appeared to me to be as impossible as if an historian of this council were not to mention one word of his holiness Pius IX. [Several voices – 'Silence, heretic, silence.'] Calm yourselves, my brethren, I have not yet finished. Forbidding me to go on, you show yourselves to the world to do wrong in shutting the mouth of the smallest member of this assembly.

I continue. The apostle Paul makes no mention, in any of his letters directed to the various churches, of the primacy of Peter. If this primacy had existed, if, in one word, the church had in its body a supreme head infallible in teaching, would the great apostle of the Gentiles have forgotten to mention it? What do I say? He would have written a long letter on this all-important subject. Then, as he has actually done, when the edifice of the Christian doctrine is erected, would the foundation, the key of the arch, be forgotten? Now, unless you hold that the church of the apostles was heretical (which none of us would either desire or dare to say), we are obliged to confess that the church has never been more beautiful, more pure, or more holy, than in the days when there was no pope. [Cries of, 'It is not true; it is not true.'] Let not Monsignor di Laval say, 'No,' since if any of you, my venerable brethren, should dare to think that the church which has today a pope for its head is more in the faith, more pure in its morals than the apostolic church, let him say it openly in the face of the universe, for this enclosure is the centre from which our words fly from pole to pole.

I go on. Neither in the writings of St Paul, St John, nor St James, have I found a trace or germ of the papal power. St Luke, the historian of the missionary labours of the apostles, is silent on this all-important point. The silence of these holy men, whose writings make part of the canon of the divinely inspired Scriptures, has appeared to me burdensome and impossible, if Peter had been pope, and as unjustifiable as if Thiers, writing the history of Napoleon Bonaparte, had omitted the title of emperor.

I see here before me a member of the assembly, who says, pointing at me with his finger, 'There is a schismatic bishop who has got among us under false colours.' No, no, my venerable brethren, I have not entered this august assembly as a thief, by the window, but by the door like yourselves. My title of bishop gave me a right to it, as my Christian conscience forces me to speak and to say that which I believe to be true.

What has surprised me most, and what moreover is capable of

demonstration, is the silence of St Peter. If the apostle had been what we proclaim him to be – that is, the vicar of Jesus Christ on earth – he surely would have known it; if he had known it, how is it that not once did he act as pope? He might have done it on the day of Pentecost, when he pronounced his first sermon, but did not do it; neither in the two letters directed to the church. Can you imagine such a pope, my venerable brethren, if St Peter had been pope? Now, if you wish to maintain that he was the pope, the natural consequence arises that you must maintain that he was ignorant of the fact. Now I ask whoever has a head to think and a mind to reflect, are these two suppositions possible?

To return, I say, while the apostle lived, the church never thought that there could be a pope; to maintain the contrary, all the sacred writings must be entirely ignored.

But it is said on all sides, 'Was not St Peter at Rome? Was he not crucified with his head down? Are not the pulpits in which he taught, the altars at which he said the mass, in this eternal city?' St Peter having been at Rome, my venerable brethren, rests only on tradition; but, if he had been Bishop of Rome, how can you from that episcopate prove his supremacy? Scaliger, one of the most learned of men, has not hesitated to say that St Peter's episcopate and residence at Rome ought to be classed with ridiculous legends. [Repeated cries, 'Shut his mouth, shut his mouth; make him come down from the pulpit.']

Venerable brethren, I am ready to be silent; but is it not better, in an assembly like ours, to prove all things, as the apostle commands, and to hold fast what is good? We have a dictator, before whom we – even his holiness Pius IX himself – must prostrate ourselves, and be silent and bow our heads. That dictator is history. This is not like a legend, which can be made as the potter makes his clay, but is like a diamond which cuts on the glass what cannot be cancelled. Till now I have only leant on her; and if I have found no trace of the papacy in the apostolic days, the fault is hers, not mine. Do you wish to put me into the position of one accused of falsehood? You may do it, if you can.

I hear from the right someone expressing these words: 'Thou art Peter, and on this rock I will build my church.' I will answer this objection presently, my venerable brethren; but, before doing so, I wish to present you with the result of my historical researches.

Finding no trace of the papacy in the days of the apostles, I said to myself, I shall find what I am in search of in the annals of the church. Well, I say it frankly – I have sought for a pope in the first four centuries, and I have not found him. None of you, I hope, will doubt the great authority of the holy Bishop of Hippo, the great and blessed St Augustine. This pious doctor – the honour and glory of the Catholic church, was secretary in the Council of Melvie. In the decrees of this venerable assembly are to be found these significant words – 'Whoever wills to appeal to those beyond the sea shall not be received by anyone in Africa to the communion.' The bishops of Africa acknowledged the Bishop of Rome so little that they smote with excommunication those who would have recourse to an appeal. These same bishops, in the sixth Council of Carthage, held under Aurelius, bishop of that city, wrote to Celestinus, Bishop of Rome, to warn him not to receive appeals from the bishops, priests or clerics of Africa; and that he should send no more legates or commissaries; and that he should not introduce human pride into the church.

That the Patriarch of Rome had from the earliest times tried to draw to himself all the authority is an evident fact; but it is an equally evident fact that he had not the supremacy which the Ultramontanes attribute to him. Had he possessed it, would the bishops of Africa – St Augustine first among them – have dared to prohibit the appeals of their decrees to his supreme tribunal? I confess without difficulty that the Patriarch of Rome held the first place. One of Justinian's laws says, 'Let us order, after the definition of the four Councils, that the holy pope of ancient Rome shall be the first of the bishops, and that the most high Archbishop of Constantinople, which is the new Rome, shall be the second.' 'Bow down then to the supremacy of the pope,' you will say to me. Do not run so fast to this conclusion, my venerable brethren, inasmuch as the law of Justin-

ian has written on the face of it, ' Of the order of the patriarchal sees.'
Precedence is one thing, the power of jurisdiction is another. For
example, supposing that in Florence there was an assembly of all
the bishops of the kingdom, the precedence would be given to the
Primate of Florence, as among the Easterns it would be accorded to
the Patriarch of Constantinople, as in England to the Archbishop of
Canterbury. But neither the first, not the second, nor the third, could
deduce from the position assigned to him a jurisdiction over his colleagues.

The importance of the Bishops of Rome proceeded not from a
divine power, but from the importance of the city in which they had
their seat. Monsignor Darboy (in Paris) is not superior in dignity to
the Archbishop of Avignon; but, in spite of that, Paris gives him a
consideration which he would not have, if, instead of having his
palace on the bank of the Seine, he had it on that of the Rhone. That
which is true in the religious order is the same in civil and political
matters: the Prefect of Rome is not more a prefect than one at Pisa;
but civilly and politically he has a greater importance.

I have said that from the very first centuries the Patriarch of
Rome aspired to the universal government of the church. Unfortu-
nately he very nearly reached it; but he had not succeeded assuredly
in his pretensions, for the Emperor Theodosius II made a law by
which he established that the Patriarch of Constantinople should
have the same authority as he of Rome (*Leg. cod. de sacr., etc*). The
fathers of the Council of Chalcedon put the bishops of the new and
the old Rome in the same order on all things, even ecclesiastical
(*Can. 28*). The sixth Council of Carthage forbade all the bishops to
take the title of prince of the bishops, or sovereign bishop. As for
this title of universal bishop, which the popes took later, St Gregory
I, believing that his successors would never think of adorning
themselves with it, wrote these remarkable words: 'None of my
predecessors has consented to take this profane name; for when a
patriarch gives himself the name of *Universal*, the title of Patriarch
suffers discredit. Far be it then from Christians to desire to give
themselves a title which brings discredit upon their brethren!'

The words of St Gregory are directed to his colleagues of Constantinople, who pretended to the primacy of the church. Pope Pelagius II calls John, Bishop of Constantinople, who aspired to the high priesthood, 'impious and profane'. 'Do not care,' he said, 'for the title of universal, which John has usurped illegally. Let none of the patriarchs take this profane name; for what misfortunes may we not expect, if among the priests such elements arise? They would get what has been foretold for them – He is the king of the sons of pride' (Pelagius II, *Lett. 13*). Do not these authorities prove (and I might add a hundred more of equal value), with a clearness as the sun at midday, that the first Bishops of Rome were not till much later recognized as universal bishops and heads of the church? And on the other hand, who does not know that from the year 325, in which the first Council of Nice was held, down to 580, the year of the Second Ecumenical Council of Constantinople, among more than 1,109 bishops who assisted at the first six general councils, there were not more than nineteen Western bishops? Who does not know that the councils were convoked by the emperors without informing, and sometimes against the wish of, the Bishop of Rome? – That Hosius, Bishop of Cordova, presided at the first Council of Nice, and edited the canons of it? The same Hosius presided afterwards at the Council of Sardica, excluding the legates of Julius, Bishop of Rome.

I say no more, my venerable brethren; and I come now to speak of the great argument – which you mentioned before – to establish the primacy of the Bishop of Rome by the rock (*petra*). If this were true, the dispute would be at an end; but our forefathers – and they certainly knew something – did not think of it as we do. St Cyril in his fourth book on the Trinity says, 'I believe that by the rock you must understand the unshaken faith of the apostles.' St Hilary, Bishop of Poitiers, in his second book on the Trinity says, 'The rock (*petra*) is the blessed and only rock of the faith confessed by the mouth of St Peter,' and in the sixth book of the Trinity he says, 'It is on this rock of the confession of the faith that the church is built.' 'God,' says St Jerome in the sixth book on St Matthew, has founded

His church on this rock, and it is from this rock that the apostle Peter has been named.' After him St Chrysostom says in his fifty-third homily on St Matthew, 'On this rock I will build my church – that is, on the faith of the confession.' Now, what was the confession of the apostle? Here it is – 'Thou art the Christ, the Son of the living God.' Ambrose, the holy Archbishop of Milan (on the second chapter of the Ephesians), St Basil of Seleucia, and the fathers of the Council of Chalcedon, teach exactly the same thing. Of all the doctors of Christian antiquity St Augustine occupies one of the first places for knowledge and holiness. Listen then to what he writes in his second treatise on the First Epistle of St John: 'What do the words mean, "I will build my church on this rock"? *On this faith,* on that which said, "Thou art the Christ, the Son of the living God."' In his treatise on St John we find this most significant phrase: 'On this rock which thou hast confessed I will build my church, since Christ was the rock.' The great bishop believed so little that the church was built on St Peter that he said to the people in his thirteenth sermon, 'Thou art Peter, and on this rock (*petra*) which thou hast confessed, on this rock which thou hast known, saying, "Thou art Christ, the Son of the living God," I will build my church – upon Myself, who am the Son of the living God: I will build it on Me, and not Me on thee.' That which St Augustine thought upon this celebrated passage was the opinion of all Christendom in his time.

Therefore, to resume, I establish: (1) That Jesus has given His apostles the same power that He gave to St Peter. (2) That the apostles never recognized in St Peter the vicar of Jesus Christ and the infallible doctor of the church. (3) That St Peter never thought of being pope, and never acted as if he were pope. (4) That the councils of the first four centuries, while they recognized the high position which the Bishop of Rome occupied in the church on account of Rome, only accorded to him a pre-eminence of honour, never of power or of jurisdiction. (5) That the holy fathers in the famous passage, 'Thou art Peter, and on this rock I will build my church,' never understood that the church was built on Peter (*super Petrum*) but on the rock (*super petram*), that is, on the confession of the faith of the apostle. I conclude victoriously, with history, with reason, with logic, with good sense, and with a Christian conscience, that Jesus Christ did not confer any supremacy on St Peter and that the Bishops of Rome did not become sovereigns of the church, but only by confiscating one by one all the rights of the episcopate. [Voices – 'Silence, impudent Protestant! Silence!']

No, I am not an impudent Protestant. History is neither Catholic, nor Anglican, nor Calvinistic, nor Lutheran, nor Arminian, nor schismatic Greek nor Ultramontane. She is what she is – that is, something stronger than all confessions of faith of the canons of the ecumenical councils. Write against it, if you dare, but you cannot destroy it, any more than taking a brick out of the Coliseum would make it fall. If I have said anything which history proves to be false, show it to me by history, and without a moment's hesitation I will make an honourable apology; but be patient, and you will see that I have not said all that I would or could; and even were the funeral pile waiting for me in the place of St Peter's, I should not be kept silent, and I am obliged to go on. Monsignor Dupanloup, in his celebrated *Observations* on this council of the Vatican, has said, and with reason, that if we declared Pius IX infallible, we must necessarily, and from natural logic, be obliged to hold that all his predecessors were also infallible.

Well, venerable brethren, here history raises its voice to assure us that some popes have erred. You may protest against it or deny it, as you please, but I will prove it. Pope Victor (192) first approved of Montanism, and then condemned it. Marcellinus (296-303) was an idolater. He entered into the temple of Vesta, and offered incense to the goddess. You will say that it was an act of weakness; but I answer, a vicar of Jesus Christ dies rather than become an apostate. Liberius (358) consented to the condemnation of Athanasius, and made a profession of Arianism, that he might be recalled from his exile and reinstated in his see. Honorius (625) adhered to Monothelitism: Father Gratry has proved it to demonstration. Gregory I (785-90) calls anyone Antichrist who takes the name of Universal Bishop, and contrariwise Boniface III (607-8) made the parricide

Emperor Phocas confer that title upon him. Paschal II (1088-99) and Eugenius III (1145-53) authorized duelling; Julius II (1509) and Pius IV (1560) forbade it. Eugenius IV (1431-39) approved of the Council of Basle and the restitution of the chalice to the church of Bohemia; Pius II (1458) revoked the concession. Hadrian II (867-872) declared civil marriages to be valid; Pius VII (1800-23) condemned them. Sixtus V (1585-90) published an edition of the Bible, and by a bull recommended it to be read; Pius VII condemned the reading of it. Clement XIV (1700-21) abolished the order of the Jesuits, permitted by Paul III, and Pius VII re-established it.

But why look for such remote proofs? Has not our holy father here present, in his bull which gave the rules for this council, in the event of his dying while it was sitting, revoked all that in past times may be contrary to it, even when that proceeds from the decisions of his predecessors? And certainly, if Pius IX has spoken *ex cathedra*, it is not when from the depths of his sepulchre he imposes his will on the sovereigns of the church. I should never finish, my venerable brethren, if I were to put before your eyes the contradictions of the popes in their teaching. If then you proclaim the infallibility of the actual pope, you must declare that the Holy Spirit has revealed to you that the infallibility of the papacy only dates from 1870. Are you bold enough to do this?

Perhaps the people may be indifferent, and pass by theological questions which they do not understand, and of which they do not see the importance; but though they are indifferent to principles, they are not so to facts. Do not then deceive yourselves. If you decree the dogma of papal infallibility, the Protestants, our adversaries, will mount in the breach, the more bold that they have history on their side, whilst we have only our own denial against them. What can we say to them when they show up all the Bishops of Rome from the days of Luke to his Holiness Pius IX? Ah! If they had all been like Pius IX, we should triumph on the whole line; but, alas! it is not so. [Cries of 'Silence, silence; enough, enough!']

Do not cry out, Monsignori! To fear history is to own yourselves conquered and, moreover, if you made the whole waters of the Tiber pass over it, you would not cancel a single page. Let me speak, and I will be as short as it is possible on this most important subject. Pope Vigilius (538) purchased the papacy from Belisarius, lieutenant of the Emperor Justinian. It is true that he broke his promise and never paid for it. Is this a canonical mode of binding on the tiara? The second Council of Chalcedon had formally condemned it. In one of its canons you read that 'The Bishop who obtains his episcopate by money shall lose it and be degraded.' Pope Eugenius III [IV in original] (1145) imitated Vigilius. St Bernard, the bright star of his age, reproves the pope, saying to him, 'Can you show me in this great city of Rome anyone who would receive you as pope if they had not received gold or silver for it?'

My venerable brethren, will a pope who establishes a bank at the gates of the temple be inspired by the Holy Spirit? Will he have any right to teach the church infallibly? You know the history of Formosus too well for me to add to it. Stephen XI caused his body to be exhumed, dressed in his pontifical robes; he made the fingers which he used for giving the benediction to be cut off, and then had him thrown into the Tiber, declaring him to be a perjurer and illegitimate. He was then imprisoned by the people, poisoned and strangled. Look how matters were readjusted; Romanus, successor of Stephen, and after him John X, rehabilitated the memory of Formosus.

But you will tell me these are fables, not history. Fables! Go, Monsignori, to the Vatican library and read Platina, the historian of the papacy, and the annals of Baronius (A.D. 897). These are facts which, for the honour of the holy see, we should wish to ignore; but when it is to define a dogma which may provoke a great schism in our midst, the love which we bear to our venerable mother church, catholic, apostolic and Roman, ought it to impose silence on us?

I go on. The learned Cardinal Baronius, speaking of the papal court, says (give attention, my venerable brethren, to these words), 'What did the Roman church appear in those days? How infamous! Only all-powerful courtesans governing in Rome! It was they who gave, exchanged and took bishoprics; and, horrible to relate, they got their lovers, the false popes, put on the throne of St Peter' (Baronius, A.D. 912). You will answer, 'These were false popes, not true ones.' Let it be so; but in that case, if for fifty years the see of Rome was occupied by anti-popes, how will you pick up again the thread of pontifical succession? Has the church been able, at least for a century and a half, to go on without a head, and find itself acephalous?

Look now: the greatest number of these anti-popes appear in a genealogical tree of the papacy; and it must have been this absurdity that Baronius described; because Genebrardo, the great flatterer of the popes, had dared to say in his *Chronicles* (A.D. 901), 'This century is unfortunate, as for nearly 150 years the popes have fallen from all the virtues of their predecessors and have become apostates rather than apostles.' I can understand how the illustrious Baronius must have blushed when he narrated the acts of these Roman bishops. Speaking of John XI (931), natural son of Pope Sergius and of Marozia, he wrote these words in his annals: 'The holy church, that is, the Roman, has been vilely trampled on by such a monster.' John XII (956), elected pope at the age of eighteen through the influence of courtesans, was not one whit better than his predecessor.

I grieve, my venerable brethren, to stir up so much filth. I am silent on Alexander VI, father and lover of Lucretia; I turn away from John XXII (1319), who denied the immortality of the soul, and was deposed by the holy Ecumenical Council of Constance. Some will maintain that this council was only a private one; let it be so; but if you refuse any authority to it, as a logical sequence you must hold the nomination of Martin V (1417) to be illegal. What, then, will become of the papal succession? Can you find the thread of it?

I do not speak of the schisms which have dishonoured the church. In those unfortunate days the see of Rome was occupied by two competitors, and sometimes even by three. Which of these was the true pope? Resuming once more, again I say, if you decree the infallibility of the present Bishop of Rome, you must establish the infallibility of the all the preceding ones, without excluding any. But can you do that, when history is there establishing with a clearness equal to that of the sun that the popes have erred in their teaching? Could you do it and maintain that avaricious, incestuous, murdering, simoniacal popes have been vicars of Jesus Christ? Oh, venerable brethren, to maintain such an enormity would be to betray Christ worse than Judas! It would be to throw dirt in His face. [Cries, 'Down from the pulpit, quick; shut the mouth of the heretic!']

My venerable brethren, you cry out; but would it not be more dignified to weigh my reasons and my proofs in the balance of the sanctuary? Believe me, history cannot be made over again; it is there, and will remain to all eternity, to protest energetically against the dogma of papal infallibility. You may proclaim it unanimously; but one vote will be wanting, and that is mine! Monsignori, the true and faithful have their eyes on us, expecting from us a remedy for the innumerable evils which dishonour the church: will you deceive them in their hopes? What will not our responsibility before God be, if we let this solemn occasion pass which God has given us to heal the true faith? Let us seize it, my brethren; let us arm ourselves with a holy courage; let us make a violent and generous effort; let us turn to the teaching of the apostles, since without that we have only errors, darkness and false traditions. Let us avail ourselves of our reason and of our intelligence to take the apostles and prophets as our only infallible masters with reference to the question of questions: 'What must I do to be saved?' When we have decided that, we shall have laid the foundation of our dogmatic system firm and immovable on the rock, lasting and incorruptible, of the divinely inspired Holy Scriptures. Full of confidence, we will go before the world and, like the apostle Paul, in the presence of the free-thinkers, we will 'know none other than Jesus Christ, and Him crucified'. We will conquer through the preaching of 'the folly of the cross', as Paul conquered the learned men of Greece and Rome; and the Roman church will have its glorious '89. [Clamorous cries, 'Get down! Out with the Protestant, the Calvinist, the traitor of the church.'] Your cries, Monsignori, do not frighten me. If my words are hot, my head is cool. I am neither of Luther, nor of Calvin, nor of Paul, nor of Apollos, but of Christ. [Renewed cries, 'Anathema, anathema, to the apostate.']

Anathema? Monsignori, anathema? You know well that you are not protesting against me, but against the holy apostles under whose protection I should wish this council to place the church. Ah! If wrapped in their winding-sheets they came out of their tombs, would they speak a language different from mine? What would you say to them when by their writings they tell you that the papacy had deviated from the gospel of the Son of God, which they have preached and confirmed in so generous a manner by their blood? Would you dare say to them, 'We prefer the teaching of our own popes, our Bellarmine, our Ignatius Loyola, to yours?' No, no! A thousand times, no, unless you have shut your ears that you may not hear, closed your eyes that you may not see, blunted your mind that you may not understand. Ah! If He who reigns above wishes to punish us, making His hand fall heavy on us, as He did on Pharaoh, He has no need to permit Garibaldi's soldiers to drive us away from the eternal city. He has only to let them make Pius IX a god, as we have made a goddess of the blessed virgin. Stop, stop, venerable brethren, on the odious and ridiculous incline on which you have placed yourselves. Save the church from the shipwreck which threatens her, asking from the Holy Scriptures alone for the rule of faith which we ought to believe and to profess. I have spoken: may God help me!

NOTES

1.   Fredrik Nielsen, *The History of the Papacy in the XIXth Century,* trans. Arthur James Mason, 2 vols (London: John Murray, 1906), II, 310.
2.   J. B. Bury, *History of the Papacy in the 19th Century,* (London: MacMillan and Co. Ltd, 1930), p.117.
3.   James Cardinal Gibbons, *A Retrospect of Fifty Years,* 2 vols, (Baltimore: James Murphy Company, 1916), I, 26.
4.   Joannes Dominicus Mansi, *Sacrorum Conciliorum Nova et Amplissima Collectio,* (Graz: Akademishe Druck – U. Verlagsanstalt, 1961), vol. 51, pp. 72-77. Also Nielsen, *op. cit.* II, 351.

5.   Gibbons, *op. cit.* I, 32.

6.   Peter Richard Kenrick, 'Speech in the Vatican Council' ed. Leonard Woolsey Bacon, *An Inside view of the Vatican Council* (New York: American Tract Society, n.d.), p. 92.

7.   *Ibid.*, p. 164.

8.   August Bernhard Hasler, *How the Pope Became Infallible* (New York: Doubleday and Company, 1981), p. 12.

9.   Lord Acton, 'The Vatican Council', H. A. MacDougal, *Lord Acton on Papal Power* (London: Sheed and Ward, 1973), p. 177.

10. *Ibid.*, p. 145.

11. James Hennesey, S. J., *The First Council of the Vatican,* (New York: Herder and Herder, 1963, p.184.

12. Dr Adrian Fortescue, 'A Slav Bishop, Joseph George Strossmayer', *Dublin Review*, October 1918, p.251.

13. Hans Kung, *The Church,* (New York: Sheed and Ward, 1967), pp. 467, 488. See also Hasler, *op. cit.* p. 176.